Headlocks and Dropkicks

Headlocks and Dropkicks

A Butt-Kicking Ride through the World of Professional Wrestling

Ted A. Kluck

PRAEGER
An Imprint of ABC-CLIO, LLC

A B C ☰ C L I O

Santa Barbara, California • Denver, Colorado • Oxford, England

Library of Congress Cataloging-in-Publication Data

Kluck, Ted.
    Headlocks and dropkicks : a butt-kicking ride through the world of professional wrestling /
    Ted A. Kluck.
       p. cm.
    Includes bibliographical references and index.
    ISBN 978–0–313–35481–6 (hard copy : alk. paper) — ISBN 978–0–313–35482–3 (ebook) 1.
Wrestling—History. I. Title.
GV1195.K48   2009
796.812—dc22   2009011688

13 12 11 10 9   1 2 3 4 5

This book is also available on the World Wide Web as an eBook.
Visit www.abc-clio.com for details.

ABC-CLIO, LLC
130 Cremona Drive, P.O. Box 1911
Santa Barbara, California 93116-1911

This book is printed on acid-free paper ∞

Manufactured in the United States of America

For The Beezer—here's to our childhood.

But there can be no real compassion for fictions on the stage. A man listening to a play is not called upon to help the sufferer; he is merely invited to feel sad.

—The Confessions of Saint Augustine

Contents

Acknowledgments

All acknowledgments on this project must begin and end with my wife, Kristin, who as a little girl probably never dreamed of marrying a guy who would spend any amount of time participating in or caring about professional wrestling. She showed a great deal of endurance, and a top-shelf sense of humor through this whole thing.

Ditto for my parents, who mostly pretended this project didn't exist; my aunt Linda, and my cousin Brian, for whom this book was written.

Thanks to Andrew, my agent, for not dropping me when I suggested this project. You rock. Ditto for Daniel Harmon and the fine folks at Praeger Publishing.

Thanks to Josh Abercrombie, a talented young wrestler, a very intelligent guy, and a patient, dutiful wrestling teacher. I was probably your worst student, but I appreciate your good interviews and fair treatment. Ditto for Mark Pennington and the rest of the Price of Glory/Michigan Sports Camps crew. You guys run a top-notch facility that I would recommend to anyone interested in the wrestling business. Thanks also to Rick Jenig, PL Myers, Jay Phoenix and all of the workers at Pro Championship Wrestling in Chicago. You're a great bunch of guys, and I appreciate the access and training.

Thanks to Joe Villa at WWE for the tickets, and for reading my first book, to Jim and Bonnie Raschke for the great interview, to Sunny Sytch for finally granting the interview, and to Leapin' Lanny Poffo for returning my call so quickly and for sharing your own writing dreams. Thanks also to Nikita Koloff for being sincere, in a world of fakes.

Big thanks to Michael Chen and Jim Olson for top notch photographs of *The LWA Presents Pride and Prejudice*. Thanks to Lan Chen and Jenny Olson for letting your husbands attend said event, and take said sweet photographs.

A huge thanks goes to J. R. Grulke, Linzo Grulke, Nick Jarmo, Pat Kelley, Charlie McMasters, and Evan Chisolm; without whom the Literary Wrestling Alliance would have just remained a bad idea, rather than become a bad idea that was acted upon and ended up being really fun. Thanks for letting an older guy act young again. Ditto for Nick Vandermolen, whose enthusiasm and passion for wrestling was infectious, and without whom I probably would have tired of this book before it was actually finished. Remember me when you're famous.

INTRODUCTION

The Genesis of Perhaps the Worst Idea I've Ever Had

I was too nervous to watch. The event was Wrestlemania III, taking place on March 29, 1987, in a far-flung, exotic venue called the Pontiac Silverdome in Pontiac, Michigan. The Silverdome, on this evening, held over 93,000 people. I imagined, in my prepubescent way, that Pontiac was a thriving city filled with beautiful women who all wore tight sweaters and thought that wrestling was real. Oh, if such a modern-day Valhalla existed! It would be several years before I actually went to Pontiac and discovered lots of strip malls, Chinese take-out places, and auto-parts stores.

I was nervous because the main event, viewable only by pay-per-view, would feature two of my childhood heroes, Hulk Hogan and Andre the Giant wrestling—horror of horrors—each other. I could not stomach the fact that at the end of the night, one of these great men would have to go home a loser. They were great men largely because they were just larger and more muscular than the rest of society. That, and they were confident. This, to a fourth-grader lacking in both musculature and confidence, was enough to elevate one to hero status.

So I waited, sequestered in my grandfather's bedroom reading wrestling magazines while my older, much worldlier cousin Brian sat in gramps' recliner and watched the events of the evening unfold.

"Hogan just slammed him!" he would shout back every now and then. Followed by something like "Andre's over the ropes!"

Brian archived his wrestling magazines in a black Hefty garbage bag. Even to my untrained fourth-grade eye, I could tell that they were cut-rate, crappily produced rags when compared to their slicker, glossier NFL and NBA brethren. They were all the same—full-color cover, with newsprint pages featuring badly written prose by guys with pen names like "Crowbar" and "Death Blow." There were always a number of black-and-white photos featuring stars like Billy Graham, Ted DiBiase, The British Bulldogs, Magnificent Muraco, The Iron Sheik (wrestling was wildly incorrect, politically), Junk Yard Dog, and others. The pictures captured high-flying action from other exotic venues such as Sioux Falls, South Dakota, and Peoria, Illinois. The wrestling circuit. By the grace of God, these were places I would see, before it was all said and done.

****

Brian is 33 years old now, and is chain smoking Marlboro Reds at his mother's breakfast nook. He builds skyscrapers for a living in downtown Chicago. After much digging in the basement, he has produced two official World Wrestling Federation–licensed rubber action figures—Muraco and Brutus "The Barber" Beefcake, left over from our childhood. We stare slack-jawed at the cartoonish figures, taken back momentarily to a past without jobs, high blood pressure, mortgages, and moral ambiguity. Good guys were good guys (or "faces," as they're known in the business) and bad guys were bad guys. I remember the large rubber figures, and their ring, being the only toys that I truly coveted as a child.

"I'm thinking about writing a wrestling book," I tell the group, which includes Brian, his girlfriend, my aunt, and my wife.

My aunt replies immediately with something that communicates what a great idea it is. But she is so unwavering in her support that I could write a book about cannibalism, or the Republican Party, and she would think it was a great idea. My wife, however, stares down at her cup of coffee and suggests that wrestling is, maybe, a little lowbrow—with which, of course, I agree 100 percent, but which is also why I think I want to do it, being a little worn out with things that aren't lowbrow. All of that to say, I want to feel some of the enthusiasm I felt as a 10-year-old wrestling fan, which is a not-unhealthy desire. Or maybe I just wish I was 10 again, which is probably unhealthy.

I'm thinking about wrestling myself, I hear myself telling the group. I have just finished a season of professional arena football, miraculously in one piece, in which my wife followed me to a bunch of loud, poorly lit Midwestern arenas in places like Battle Creek, Port Huron, and Marion. The last thing she wants to endure is another year full of even smaller, seedier venues filled with more opportunities for injuries and even weirder people. I'll take a few lessons, I tell them. Maybe wrestle a real match.

****

I couldn't say, exactly, why I want to train to become a professional wrestler for a match or two. I like the fact that it's fake, or, more accurately, that the outcomes are predetermined; unlike in arena football, where my mistakes could cost us games and maybe even cost teammates and coaches their jobs. I also like the idea of an alter ego—one with swagger and moxie, two things I have never had in abundance.

I held on to Rich Jenig's[1] number for a while, and just let it sit on my office desk, shifting it around occasionally while I finished up other projects. It would appear frequently under a pile of bills, or on top of a stack of notebooks. I looked at his Web site—scanning through the pictures of his training facility and wrestling shows that took place in civic auditoriums and high school gymnasiums. The promotions had names like "New Years Evil" at the Midlothian Civic Auditorium and "Thanksgiving Turmoil" at the American Legion Hall in Summit, Illinois.

Truth be told, I already have my handle worked out before I dial Rich Jenig. I have been batting different ideas around in my mind—keeping them to myself, of course. I am settling on "Professor Pain" or "The Great American Author." I'll wear a tweed sportsjacket into the ring, and smoke a pipe. My finishing move will be something called the "tenure track" or the "final exam."

Jenig has a thick Chicago accent, to go along with the raspy voice of the smoker, or of one who has a day job but spends most of the rest of his tired waking hours pursuing a passion. Before sharing the idea, we spend several moments talking about family connections, and

---

[1] Jenig is a distant cousin who runs a long-standing, successful wrestling promotion in Chicago.

reminiscing about my grandfather—who was his great uncle. "I had breakfast with that guy once a month for years!" he says, of "Turk," my gramps. I feel a pang of jealousy, momentarily, that he lived close enough to gramps to do that.

He has heard about my first book, *Facing Tyson,* through another family member, which bodes well for this idea. I move into my pitch —a pitch I had used at least once before, with the *Paper Tiger* concept. Although this, somehow, seemed a little bit more ridiculous, perhaps because I had never wrestled, or considered wrestling before.

Jenig is surprisingly receptive. He invites me to visit his wrestling school any time, and that he would be more than willing to allow me to train for the purposes of a book. He tells me his philosophy on wrestling—that it's for the kids, for entertainment, and that he would like to get back to a form of professional wrestling that is more about fun characters and less about seedy storylines.

"I've only got three rules at my wrestling school," he explains. "No drugs. Everybody gets along. Nobody gets hurt.

"There's really no average student," he says of the school, which also puts on a show in the area each month. "I've got guys with master's degrees, and guys who are borderline retarded. But I get kids coming in here all the time with stars in their eyes, thinking they're going to be on television, and I explain that if they aren't in college in three months, they're fired."

He then goes on to paint a wholly unflattering picture of aging wrestlers, a group of which he is a part. "Most of them are broke as a joke," he says. "If they don't piss it[2] away on drugs, the divorce usually gets them. Hell, Lex Luger is living in a church basement now."[3] Luger was a huge WWE star in the 80s and early 90s, and his cautionary tale is not unlike many of those I encountered in my research for *Facing Tyson.*

I hang up the phone, feeling oddly excited—a feeling which comes less and less frequently in adulthood. I get excited about time with my wife, a good meal out, Tristan seeing his grandparents, etc. But unbridled, childlike excitement is hard to come by.

---

[2]Money, that is.

[3]At the time, I feel like Jenig is just being unnecessarily brash or negative, but it only takes a little bit of research to discover that he's absolutely right.

Before flipping the light off in my office and wrapping up for the evening, I stop by a mirror on the way out, catching a reflection. I suck in my gut and flex a little bit, but only after looking down the hallway to make sure there is no one there to see me.

****

My most startling wrestling discovery is the fact that anticipating the wrestling was better than actually doing/experiencing the wrestling. Simply put, this was a funner book to talk about than to actually do, which any middle-ager who has ever experienced the axiom that "wanting is more satisfying than getting" could have told me up front. That, though, is one of the dilemmas of the adult who is into, or tries for a time to be into, wrestling: It's for kids. Despite the fact that wrestling has gone through its scantily-clad-women-and-seedy-storylines phases, it's still something, like amusement parks, that I equate with childhood, and that I quickly discovered will never be as fun as it was then.

I also realized after writing the last few sentences that this is a book that will probably satisfy almost nobody. Most wrestling books are either so kayfabey as to be directed toward adolescents or barely functional adults, or they're so tongue-in-cheek, been-there-done-that cynical as to only appeal to a very narrow wrestling-Internet-journal-reading, know-everything-already demographic that is obsessed with new, gossipy bits of learned information such as who was on steroids and who was screwing whom (both literally and figuratively).

This book, of course, is neither. I equate it more to a documentary film. The discovery, for me, came in doing it. In realizing that most wrestlers, like most men in any job or field, are world-weary, cynical, and exhausted. That they don't feel like superheroes and may or may not have even had that much fun doing what they were doing. I feel like I knew this on a head level, going in, but finding out that it was true was still a blow. In one sense, I expected the wrestlers to be like the boxers I profiled in *Facing Tyson*, who were still, to a man, full-time dreamers who truly believed that fame, fortune, and happiness were just one more fight away. *Facing Tyson* was a spiritually enriching experience, while this, I'm afraid, was more proof that life is difficult, people are lonely, and sometimes it's hard to feel genuine excitement.

The real fun in this book was in the anticipation and the community. It was reading wrestling magazines and going to shows with Brian, or watching videos with J. R., Vandermolen, and Jarmo. It was talking about wrestling while our wives and girlfriends rolled their eyes. Planning characters. Conceiving magazines. Cutting promos. Designing T-shirts. It was in being obsessed, for a season, with something we knew was just that—a season that would have a finite beginning and end point before we all moved on and, hopefully, grew up.

CHAPTER 1

Michigan Sports Camps and the Price of Glory

The gym is ambiguously named "Michigan Sports Camps," which calls to mind images of a shimmering lake, volleyball nets, free time, lunch, and perhaps some softball. What I'm seeing is anything but. Michigan Sports Camps is actually an out-building behind UFC legend and former WWE superstar Dan "The Beast" Severn's home in Cold-water, Michigan. All former WWE wrestlers, it seems, are referred to as superstars, as though simply making it to the WWE implies super-star status.[1] Michigan Sports Camps houses several immaculately kept wrestling rings, boxing rings, wrestling mats, and a large weight room. This is where Severn teaches men of all ages the finer points of beating each other up.

When I meet Severn, he is sweeping up around the rings. "I'm president, CEO, and janitor," he says, extending a thick hand that has choked, beaten, maimed, and pinned all over the world. I can't say the gym is what you might expect, because I have no idea what to expect. Movies like the *Rocky* series gave us some idea that these sorts of gyms were dank, depressing hovels where broken-down men trained to break each other down even more.

I have brought along a sidekick for the occasion—a friend named Nick, who I am trying to convince to take the professional wrestling

---

[1]Not exactly true.

classes with me. Nick is short and soft—a short-story writer/performance artist. He has on a jacket that says something like "Peterson Snow Removal," though he has never worked, I'm sure, in snow removal. Nick once staged a fashion show in which all of the models wore clothes made out of garbage, and he ended the event by stripping down to a burlap sack, having all of his back hair shaven off, and belly flopping into a large fountain. "Like all art, the symbolism and metaphor is different for everybody," he said after the Garbage installation. Not surprisingly, given that information, Nick is also a huge wrestling fan. He hosts *Monday Night Raw* parties in his apartment that have become the stuff of legend. Lots of energy drinks, shirtlessness, broken coffee tables, etc.

Nick and I have been discussing character names and possible tag-team options for ourselves should this thing materialize. He's decided on a character called The Best Man, as he is in several weddings this year. The idea being that he would wear a hideous tuxedo into the ring before stripping down to a pair of cringe-inducing wrestling briefs. For our tag-team effort, we've decided on The English Department as a moniker.

Dan Severn sports the kind of moustache that was made popular by police officers and male adult film actors in the 1980s. However, I'm not about to make light of that fact, because, quite frankly, I find Severn a little terrifying. Having interviewed lots of men who fight for a living, they all have an indefinable bit of "crazy" to them, and Severn is no exception.

In 1996, he was crowned the Ultimate Fighting Championships Superfight Champion, and then later won something called the Ultimate Ultimate, in which he fought and beat up champions from other organizations back when the sport's only rules prohibited biting and eye gouging. I am relieved to learn, today, that groin shots are now illegal. Score one for progress.

We are taken on a fast tour of the facility by Mark Pennington, now a full-time employee of Michigan Sports Camps, who was once a student in Severn's professional wrestling course.

"I had worked three straight years of retail jobs after I graduated high school, and I just needed something. You could call it a life crossroads at age 21. I got mixed up in the mythology of WCW and WWF, as they were trading guys in that 1998 era," says Pennington. "I wanted to be on TV. I wanted to be an actor or an entertainer. I wanted to be involved in whatever capacity may come. So I came here and watched a practice and was mesmerized by everything they were doing . . . but of course my situation was different because I had a wife and child."

I stop Pennington, to commiserate. "I'm writing a wrestling book" are perhaps the last words a wife wants to hear, followed closely by "and I'm going to wrestle."

"She (Pennington's wife) realized I had changed for the better . . . I had purpose after I started wrestling," he says. "I was working at Wal-Mart, stocking shelves and when I found wrestling I wasn't just living to live. I had no athletic background at all. I did nothing. I wasn't in great shape but I went through the process anyway. The first two weeks are a huge mental game. Your body is processing so much that it's not used to. You've got to do your bumps in training. We're very safe here, and we've got crash pads and everything like that, so we make sure that guys are comfortable before they start doing something. But that first week driving home, it was like 'Oh man this sucks so bad.' "

****

Josh Abercrombie is smaller than I expected. He is the professional wrestling instructor at Michigan Sports Camps, and is perhaps the state of Michigan's hottest independent wrestling personality. He joins us dressed in a pair of pajama pants and a T-shirt with "LuchaDork" emblazoned across the chest.

Abercrombie teaches wrestling here two nights a week, and wrestles throughout the Midwest on Friday, Saturday, and Sunday of every week. His matches are marked by his high-flying "spots" which have Abercrombie often hurtling over the top rope and into the chairs and people that sit at ringside. This willingness to sacrifice his 5′9″ body has drawn favorable comparisons to Rey Mysterio and has given Abercrombie the opportunity to wrestle in Canada, Germany, and Mexico.

Abercrombie works as a heel (bad guy) most nights, explaining that "it's just easier for me, I guess." His character is a sort of preppie emo-kid who oozes the confidence that comes from being better than everybody. In short, he's a hateable prick in the ring.

"As long as I can remember, I wanted to be a professional wrestler," says Abercrombie, who wrestled competitively in high school. "I kind of got my training piecemeal from different guys. I was big into the tape-trading scene[2] back in the late 1990s and another guy, who now wrestles as The Old Timer Jeff King, contacted me and told me about a guy with a wrestling school in Grand Rapids. I was fifteen years old at the time and I borrowed my mom's car and drove it illegally to GR so that I could train with this guy. It ended up being the most unsafe place . . . this guy had us doing insane powerbombs and stuff on the first day.

"I learned to take bumps from Frankie the Face,"[3] he continued, "and Matt Maverick—who wrestles as Bloody Harker Dirge—has a ring at his place so he was a huge help in getting me started."

Abercrombie wrestled his first match at age 17, in a ring set up outside a bar. "I was wearing a mask," he adds. He has longish hair, with a three-day scruff on his young face and dark circles under his eyes. Abercrombie is probably in his mid-twenties now and is married to wrestling. He has a girlfriend who is set to graduate from college and get a job, but he shows no signs of settling down. He sees his friends graduating from college as well, and getting lucrative office jobs around the state; however the pull of wrestling is still too much for him.

"My family always asks when I'm going to get married and settle down," he says. "But I have no intention of doing that. I have no intention of giving up right now."

In addition to the wrestling, Abercrombie makes his living as a special education assistant in a local high school. His job is to follow discipline-problem and special-needs kids through the school day, and take care of any incidents that may occur. He looks exhausted. I ask about health insurance.

"I don't have health insurance," he explains. "I thought I broke my neck once, which was scary, and one time I ruptured my eardrum in a match. I got a fake address off the Internet—I'm good at memorizing numbers and things—and filled out the paperwork at one of these walk-in-type clinics. I told the guy I got hit in the ear playing touch football and he wrote me a prescription for antibiotics and Vicodin. I gave them my Social Security number with the last few numbers backwards. I only had 25 bucks to my name at the time, and I called another wrestler who

---

[2]Unbeknownst to me, there was a "scene" for this, and when Abercrombie says "tape trading," he means tapes of wrestling shows—ostensibly, the more obscure, the better.

[3]Wrestlers often refer to other wrestlers by their ring names, which takes some getting used to. Later in the book, I meet a newlywed wife, who introduces her wrestler husband to me as "Whiplash."

was willing to give me $60 for the Vicodin, so I was able to get the anti-biotics I needed to fix my ear. I told him I'd give him 30 Vicodin for 40 bucks. That's the kind of stuff that happens."

Injuries certainly do happen in wrestling, which is one of my apprehensions with this project. The warnings at the beginning of each WWE video are especially grisly—showing people flying off ladders, crashing through tables, and then being carried off on stretches in various states of broken/bleeding for real. The videos are all accompanied with a message along the lines of "No matter what you do, don't try this at home." This is especially nerve-wracking for me, because "trying this" is exactly what I'm here to do. Abercrombie is a living example of the toll-taking nature of the sport at the independent level. He is almost always injured, and almost never has a day off.

"I was off Friday—which was great—and went to see [the] Bee movie ... my girlfriend is into those kids' cartoon movies," he explains. "And then I wrestled in Indianapolis on Saturday, in a three-way dance[4] and then in Joliet, Illinois, on Sunday."

Abercrombie has flown to Mexico once, where he received $400 to wrestle, and has also flown to Germany, but most of his work is of the Midwestern, car-trip variety. I am nervous to ask him how much wrestlers make for these local, Indy gigs.

"My first real, pro match was against the Old Timer Jeff King and we were each paid $30 which covered half of our gas and beer for the trip," he says. "Honestly, the average Indy guy is a gas-money maker. The problem is, you're afraid to ask for money because there are so many guys who will do this for next to nothing."

****

Abercrombie is in the ring now, instructing his young charges and taking abuse from a Mexican boxer who was training in one of the other rooms in the labyrinthine training facility. The Mexican boxer is strutting around shirtless, flexing for a middle-aged woman and her daughter who are sitting on a bench at ringside.

"Abercrombie, you always wear your nightclothes into the ring?" he says, mocking Abercrombie's cotton pants. "Yo man, check this out." He produces a cellular phone and calls up several compromising photos of a young woman who shared his company recently. He and

---

[4]This is a match in which three guys wrestle at once, and the first guy to pin somebody wins.

Abercrombie share the universal raised eyebrows and nods that seem to communicate something like "Yes, I went out with her, and yes, she is as hot as she looks."

"She cried when I left," explains the Mexican boxer, "but I told her I had to go beat someone's ass." A touching sentiment from a man who currently lives in a bunkbed. Abercrombie reminds the boxer to watch his language because there are "like a hundred" women in the room, and eventually he wanders off.

Abercrombie is working with two aspiring wrestlers in the ring: Louis Kendrick, a former gymnast who has been training for two months, and Bryan Whitmore, who last year was a high school wrestler. Kendrick, a pure acrobat, handles the high-flying move combinations easily. He is working on launching himself into the ring, taking a bump, and then running diagonally to the opposite turnbuckle, into which he slams full speed. From this distance—ringside—I gain a new appreciation for how hard the athletes are actually hitting the ring floor. The ring is designed to make noise under their weight, but they are still hitting it hard. As they arm-drag each other into the mat, Abercrombie encourages them to "sell" their pain.

"Take a minute and stay down, let it register," he explains. "If you hit a concrete parking lot like that you would stay down. If you would stay down if you hit the ground, stay down here."

Abercrombie produces a giant three-ring binder, filled with the various "spots" he has accumulated over the years. "I worked with another wrestler named 'The Hype' Jimmy Shalwin, who would record all his spots, and he was very meticulous about it," he says. "Eventually, I started doing it. It's not like I sit down with the book and plan out every aspect of every match, but if something happens in a match that I like, I'll type it out and add it to the book."

He explains that typically he only has a few minutes to go over spots with his opponents on the road. "Usually I have no idea who I'm wrestling until I get to the venue," he says. "On the road it's all about putting asses in the seats, so the promoter lets us know who he wants to win, and it's usually the local guy. I'm most likely going to be a heel on the road, too. But I like being the heel, because I'm more in control of the match that way."

I ask Abercrombie how he communicates with his opponent during the match. "There's a lot of communication the audience doesn't see," he says. "Like when I have a guy in a headlock, and the crowd can't see his mouth moving, that's a great time to have a conversation or talk about next moves. Or when you're on the mat grappling with a guy, you can just give him a 'squeeze and if he squeezes back, he's okay . . . and if he doesn't he needs a little more time to recover."

We both agree that what wrestling needs is a greater variety of well-developed characters but, unfortunately, what it has instead is a bunch of 6′3 230″ pound, "jacked-up"[5] drones. Gone, too, are the days of characters, good and bad, based on ethnicity.[6]

"You would never see an American Dream Dusty Rhodes today," he laments. "But that was a great character . . . he was the everyman. You probably wouldn't even see a Nature Boy Ric Flair or a Harley Race. Flair is nothing special physically, and Harley has a big belly on him. Flair was the perfect villain because he played that 'pampered rich kid' role so well. I got to meet Harley Race once after a show I wrestled down South. He came to the locker room afterward, shook my hand and told me 'that's why I can barely walk anymore.' It was a huge honor."

****

Abercrombie has given his students five minutes to talk through the "spots" in a seven-minute match they will conduct in the ring, without touching or using the ropes.

"I'm gonna be Bill Watts[7] tonight," Abercrombie says. He then leans over the ropes to explain to Nick and me, "It's important to know you're wrestling history." Whitmore has chosen to be the "heel" (bad

---

[5]Jacked up, in Abercrombie's vernacular, refers to guys whose physiques are big and ripped, due mostly to the help of anabolic steroids.

[6]I'm thinking specifically of characters like the Iron Sheik, who played upon America's fear of Middle Easterners, and Nikolai Volkoff, who was the quintessential Russian bad guy throughout his career, though he didn't actually hail from Russia and is now a small-time politician in Maryland. Volkoff would whip American crowds into a frenzy by singing the Russian national anthem in the middle of the ring before each match. See also: Mr. Fuji, Kamala the Ugandan Giant, The Sheikh (different from the Iron Sheik, but similar). On the unchecked patriotism side, see Hacksaw Jim Duggan and Sergeant Slaughter as well as Hulk Hogan's use of the song *I am a Real American,* which played while he was walking into the ring and ripping off his T-shirt. Come to think of it, an unbelievable number of WWF storylines dealt with beating up foreigners, which would never fly today but, looking back, was pretty harmless and probably more innocent than some of the misogynistic storylines that dominated wrestling in the 1990s.

[7]Watts is a former pro wrestler and promoter, most recently working as the executive vice president of WCW (World Championship Wrestling), from which he resigned in 1992. He was replaced by Eric Bischoff. Watts was known for his affinity for grappling and his disdain for wrestlers using the ropes to perform high spots.

guy) tonight and enters the ring sporting a "Johnny Heisman" persona. He shouts, "Whose house? My house!" repeatedly, and strikes the Heisman Trophy pose before entering the ring. Kendrick, the "face" (good guy), goes with a kung-fu routine in which he performs a front flip over the top rope and starts gyrating around the ring, kung-fu style. In many ways, this is an interesting peek behind the curtain, as both wrestlers are without many of the flashy accessories that help them put a character "over." The room is quiet as they work, and the only audible sounds are the thuds of feet and bodies on the mat. Nick and I glance at each other often as bodies crash against the ring floor—this stuff is going to hurt. Abercrombie continues to urge his charges to "sell" the pain they're experiencing, but the manifestation of that coaching seems to just be a lot of grunting. He scribbles notes furiously on a little notepad while the two men grapple in the ring.

****

My son is five years old, and as such, his attention span is pretty short. I've tried watching football with him, and he watches for a few minutes, but it's only a matter of time before he's on the floor wriggling around, dancing, or making his toy cars explode. However, one of the perks of writing a book about professional wrestling is that "research" often involves watching wrestling tapes. Lots of wrestling tapes. I am careful to put these in when my wife is busy doing other things, so as to avoid the eye-rolls that inevitably come as she walks through the living room area.

This night I've chosen Wrestlemania III and the Ricky Steamboat vs. Randy Savage Intercontinental Title[8] match that is widely considered among the best matches in wrestling history. Before the match, there is a segment in which "The Macho Man" Randy Savage is interviewed by Mary Hart. Tristan is mesmerized by the overly fake-baked man with the shoe-leather skin and the gravely voice. Savage also wears lots of teal and neon, and has on a pair of sunglasses which manage to obscure most of his face, save for the scraggly beard and the always-moving mouth. He continually says "oh yeah" and does funny

---

[8]The Intercontinental Title is a sort of lower-tier title created mainly to provide grist for another set of storylines which often ebb and flow more often than the more prestigious World Title. Don't read much into the geographical undertones in the title, though, as the WWE used to have something called a "European Championship" that was last held by a guy from North Carolina.

things with his hands, including dropping a coffee mug which is symbolic of the "cup of coffee" that Ricky Steamboat has had in the WWE. It's a brilliant interview which manages, somehow, to be understated in spite of the teal and yelling. Tristan laughs out loud, and I think I'm closer to targeting the WWE's demographic—five-year-old boys.

The match, of course, is a beauty. It is that rare combination of wrestlers who have big bodies but are still capable of high-flying maneuvers and top-notch grappling. There is also an above-average storyline in which Savage seems to be on the outs with Elizabeth, one of the WWE's first babe valets.

"Are they really mad at each other, Daddy?" Tristan asks, as Savage ascends the top rope to drop a move on the prone Steamboat. Tris is riveted to the couch, and hasn't moved in 20 minutes. This is a personal record for him.

I mull for a moment how best to answer this question. I put it in the same category as "Is Santa Claus real?"

"Well, buddy," I explain. "What they're doing is play fighting." Yeah, play fighting. I can see the wheels spinning in his little mind. He sees them leaping and crashing into each other and into the mat, which makes a satisfying thud upon impact. It looks real, and at some level it is. It hurts to crash into a mat, whether the storylines are scripted or not. But he play fights with his friends, and this is something to which he can relate. Unfortunately, pro wrestling seems to have sold its spandex-clad soul to the 18–35 male demographic, which, if the shows are any indication, seem to clamor for nothing more than scantily clad women, loud music, and raunchy storylines. Still, the retro-ridiculousness, loud costumes, and play fighting will always find its way into the hearts of children.

"Daddy," he asks finally, "can we wrestle?" I climb down from the couch and give him a quick primer on the headlock, the elbow drob, and his favorite, the knife-edge. I then take his little legs and put him into a figure-four leglock as he laughs out loud.

CHAPTER 2

I Might as Well Be a Babyface: Leapin' Lanny Poffo

Forgiveness is the fragrance that the violet sheds upon the hell that has crushed it.

—Mark Twain

The "Wrestling on the Water" cruise is billed as including "seminars, one on one discussions, hands-on wrestling tips, and more!" and the poster features Lanny Poffo, circa "The Genius" vs. another wrestler named "Jammin' " Johnny West, who wears a leopard-print tarzan singlet and a mullet. "I needed a wrestler who wasn't going to get drunk and make a pass at a fan's wife," Poffo explains. "Johnny was the only guy I could think of."

It is a sad commentary on the business, but the cruise, Poffo's brainchild, is a way, ostensibly, for fans to get close to wrestling while enjoying all of the other amenities of cruise life. However, Poffo explains, liability has made it impossible for fans to actually get into the ring with him. "They're not going to actually let me wrestle fans," he says, "but I assured them that nobody would get hurt. I've never been hurt in all my years in wrestling, and I've never hurt anyone in the ring."

Poffo still wrestles a handful of independent shows each year, and operates under the mantra that "if the money's right, I'll be there tonight."

"My parents are 82 and 80, my brother just turned 55 and I'll turn 53 next month," he says. "My brother[1] is a little bit beat up, but he's happy and healthy, and hung on to his money."

I ask Poffo if he ever felt a sense of competition with his brother, Randy Savage, who is arguably one of a handful of the most famous wrestlers on the planet.

"I was an oversensitive kid with a bad complexion, trying to fit in with a world of men," he explains. "Randy gave me my start, and working with him over the years was 100 percent good. Vince McMahon saw a tape of my brother jumping off the top rope and onto the floor, which nobody did back then. He signed him, and Randy asked them if they had a spot for me. They said, 'Not on top.' Randy turned to me and said 'Do you want to be a face or a heel?' and I said, 'If I'm not gonna be on top, I might as well be a babyface.' "

Savage went on to collect the WWE[2] Intercontinental Heavyweight Championship and the WCW World Heavyweight Championship, among others, while Poffo carved out a smaller niche with characters like "Leapin' Lanny Poffo, the Poet Laureate of the WWE," and later, "The Genius," a heel-character that is best known for wearing academic gowns into the ring, and for a four-month feud with überchampion Hulk Hogan.

"I could be jealous of Randy,[3] or upset over what he accomplished," he says, "but that would only hurt me. What people don't realize is that it hasn't all been easy for Randy. They weren't there like I was in 1971 when Randy wasn't getting drafted in baseball, and in '75 when he was just a skinny wrestler.

"I was backstage once at a WWE show and Rick Rude came up to me and said that the only reason I was there was because of my brother," he says. "I looked at him and said, 'It is,' and everyone started to laugh. At him.

---

[1]His brother is the more famous "Macho Man" Randy Savage, whose renown was generated by his turn as one of the WWE's most successful heel characters, as well as his appearance in several "Slim Jim" beef jerky snack commercials. He was also known for his deep, raspy voice (think several packs of Marlboros per day) and the catchphrase "Ohh yeah."

[2]The WWE (World Wrestling Entertainment) used to be called the WWF (World Wrestling Federation) until the other WWF (World Wildlife Foundation) decided they didn't want to be associated with Vince McMahon and his group of spandex-clad warriors.

[3]Savage was a six-time world champion—four times in WCW and twice in WWF(E), where he held the World Championship twice and the Intercontinental title once.

"These are the types of people you have to break bread with, in wrestling," he says of Rude and his hard-partying contemporaries. "Everybody wanted to live like John Belushi, but I'd like to be a productive old man. I think I kept getting booked because I was always clean and sober."

****

Lanny Poffo, part-time wrestler, now sells cars during the day for a CarMax franchise near Tampa, Florida. He says that most of his customers have no idea that he is a former wrestling star, but that his action figure is in a trophy case in the lobby. He enjoys the car business because it plays to two of his skill sets—typing ("around 100 words a minute"), and interacting with people.

"I'll walk customers by it (the action figure) if I think it will help make a sale," he explains. "But I guess I'm trying to distance myself from that gimmick. I've cut my hair and I'm more clean cut now. I don't look anything like I did when I wrestled."

Poffo, born in 1954 in Calgary, Alberta, became a star in his father Angelo's promotion—International Championship Wrestling—where he held the title. Poffo was one of the few "high flyers" in the WWE, and though he was known mostly as a "jobber"[4] to the stars, occasionally winning a match and usually getting in a fair amount of offense. Unlike most wrestlers, for whom a gimmick is just, well, a gimmick, Poffo's true passion was, and still is, writing.

"My first big break came in the fifth grade when a teacher told me I had the ability to be a writer," he explains. "I dedicated my first book, a collection of children's limericks, to her." Poffo has become something of a crusader for smoking cessation, and the limerick book, entitled *Limericks from the Heart (and Lungs)* is described on his Web site as "a must-read for every concerned parent who wants to raise smoke-free children."[5] In 1988 Poffo self-published a book of his poems called *Wrestling with Rhyme.*

"In wrestling, I tried not to be the guy who was shouting and screaming all the time," he says, which pretty much describes everyone else in wrestling. "If they were all screaming 'kill, kill, kill,' I wanted to do the opposite.

---

[4]Jobbers are wrestlers who are brought in to "put over" or lose to bigger-named opponents that a promotion wants to promote.
[5]According to Poffo, 4,000 children start smoking each day in America.

"My second lucky break came in 1977," he says. "It was right before Elvis died, and I was wrestling in Nashville. I was approached by a man with an entourage, who wanted an autograph. I find out he's from Chicago and he's a big White Sox fan, and I tell him I'm from Downers Grove and a Cubs fan. We banter for a while, and then I realize I'm talking to Shel Silverstein! He didn't act like he was anything. I saw him again in 1991, when I was coming back from wrestling in the Dominican Republic. He was sitting in the Miami airport, alone, and I was a little shy and reluctant at first. I debated as to whether to say anything to him, and finally I approached him and said 'You came to see me wrestle back in the late-seventies . . . and my hair was different back then,' and he says "Oh, Lanny Poffo!

"After we talked for a while I finally mustered the courage to tell him about a book I was thinking about writing, and I asked him if it was a good idea. He looked at me for a minute, and he finally said, 'You know, when we first met I figured you for a pretty smart guy, but now I'm going to have to reevaluate my assessment.' I'm thinking 'Oh great, I'm going through a divorce, I feel terrible, this is all I need. Shel fucking Silverstein.[6] I ask him what he means, and he says, 'We've got freedom of speech in this country, so SPEAK!' By this time, he's shouting in the middle of an airport, which you don't do. And I'm thinking, why is this crazy old man yelling at me? But he knew I needed a nudge."

****

Poffo admits to using anabolic steroids once during his career, in 1989, when he was training for his heel turn as Hulk Hogan's arch nemesis. It was this era that provided some of the highest points of Poffo's career as a wrestler.

The Genius was similar to Poffo's early characters in many ways, namely the fact that he continued to recite poetry in the ring, but the differences contributed to the psychology behind modern heel-making. The Genius wore a pink academic cap and gown into the ring, and affected a dainty, more feminine quality in his wrestling as well as his promotional interviews. There was eye shadow. These academic

---

[6]Silverstein is one of America's most loved authors of children's books, including *The Giving Tree* and *Where the Sidewalk Ends*. He also wrote the song "A Boy Named Sue" for Johnny Cash.

and flamboyant flourishes both helped make Poffo a character that was imminently loathable by wrestling's hyper-masculinized, beer-drinking male audience.

"I am a monogamous heterosexual," The Genius intoned in 1989 on *Regis and Kathie Lee* when asked the exact nature of his relationship with Mr. Perfect, the late Curt Hennig. But the long fingernails, eye makeup and general daintiness spoke volumes. "You'd be amazed what he's got underneath that gown," said Hennig. The Genius, now, was a villain.

Poffo references his matches with Hogan often, and it's clear that their tilt in Topeka, Kansas, on NBC's Saturday Night's Main Event, was a watershed moment for him.

The Genius began the match by offering Hogan a left-handed hand-shake, and then backed away to stretch, ballet-style, in the corner. After felling Hogan with an arm-drag, Poffo pranced and pirouetted around the ring once again, much to the disdain of the crowd. Hogan, by then infinitely frustrated, attempted to takes Poffo's head off with a couple of clothleslines, and then rammed his head into each turn-buckle, much to the delight of the capacity crowd.

Poffo's most impressive maneuver was a backflip off the top rope, landing directly on top of Hogan and then covering him for a two-count. Eventually, The Genius was thrown out of the ring by Hogan, who is then attacked by Mr. Perfect. Hogan was counted out, and The Genius won the match but not the title.

The short-lived angle ultimately fell flat, I think, because it didn't allow Hogan to draw upon the hyper-patriotic, underdog ethos that powered him through his most legendary feuds (see Andre the Giant, The Iron Sheik, etc.). The crowd never believed that Hogan had any chance of actually losing to a lightweight like The Genius, so he never had a chance to get beat down, begin convulsing himself and the crowd into action, and then do the patented leg-drop finish that had become his trademark. Beating up The Genius was, for Hogan, analogous to beating up one's sister.

That era, however, and Hogan specifically, would become a light-ning rod for the steroid allegations that would plague Vince McMahon and WWE through much of the 1990s and into 2007, when WWE superstar Chris Benoit was involved in a grisly alleged murder/suicide.

This is a good time to talk about the fact that wrestler deaths are never seen or remembered as especially cool or tragic or heroic. There are no Jeff Buckleys[7] in wrestling, or even any Duane Allmans, Michael Hutchences[8], or Marc Bolans.[9] There are lots of deaths, many of which are of the steroid-related variety—and some, but fewer, are of the suicide variety. Some, like Adorable Adrian Adonis (real name Keith Franke), die doing very ordinary working-wrestlerish things like driving, which any working wrestler will tell you they've done an ungodly amount of—more than steroids, boozing, or whoring combined. Working wrestlers drive, a lot, and thus put themselves in highway-related harm's way a lot more than the rest of us. Adonis was riding in a minivan with a bunch of other wrestlers[10] driving to a show in Canada when, allegedly, the driver of the minivan swerved to avoid hitting a moose and the minivan careened into a lake.[11]

"I was a guest on *Hannity & Colmes* in the aftermath of the Chris Benoit murders," Poffo says. "Of all the people in the world, Chris was the last guy you would expect to kill his family,[12] and of course they blamed it on the wrestling business, and on steroids. But four women a day are murdered by their husbands, I did the research."

After praying about it, Poffo said he decided to come clean about his steroid use on the program. "I don't blame the sport for any of this stuff; I always think you have to blame the individual. I'm never going to point a finger at someone else, or throw anyone under the bus, but I knew that question would come up and I thought it was wisest to just own up to my use," he says. "I told them that I experienced two side effects from the steroids—facial acne and testicular atrophy. My face has cleared up, and they'll just have to take my word for the other."

Strangely, wrestlers, whose careers hinge on the art of deception, often end up being much more forthcoming about their steroid use than

---

[7]Columbia Records still maintains a Web site for Buckley, who has been deceased now for over a decade and has achieved Messiah-like fame in thoughtful music circles that probably wouldn't have come—no disrespect intended—were it not for his death.

[8]The lead singer for INXS, who hung himself from a doorknob with a standard-issue brown pants-belt.

[9]The frontman for a band called T. Rex, probably responsible for some of the worst arena-rock in sports history.

[10]Simply reading that Adonis dies riding in a minivan through Canada with a bunch of other wrestlers on the way to probably work some hellhole venue (like the Canadian version of an American Legion hall) strikes me as profoundly sad. Sadder, almost, than the death itself.

[11]This is all according to Wikipedia, so take it with a grain of salt, but still.

[12]This begs the question: Is there anyone in the world from whom you really expect this?

participants in other mainstream sports. The 2008 Major League Baseball season was the first season since MLB adopted more stringent steroid testing and a season that, not surprisingly, has seen a drastic downturn in home runs. The strapping baseballers who play America's game, and sell America trucks, beer, and financial products during the commercial breaks, seem to have a much tougher time coming clean about their substances. Rather than face the media heat, slugger Mark McGwire has basically gone underground. His colleague Barry Bonds has done the same. Ditto for Sammy Sosa. These men seem to have struck a de facto deal with the public regarding their alleged use or nonuse of performance-enhancers. Unfortunately, they'll waive the opportunity to publicly tell young people of their dangers.

The media seems to target a large quantity of their steroid-related angst in the direction of wrestling—where, let's face it, the outcomes don't matter much, if at all. It's not like Hogan's alleged steroid use taints the "legacy" of the heavyweight title. That would be like arguing that Stallone's possible use of steroids to beef up for his role in *Rocky IV* somehow taints our enjoyment of that film—which, in fact, seems like a two-hour advertisement for anabolics.

Poffo blames the media's disdain for wrestling on the success of the sport—perhaps, the fact that wrestling's politically incorrect theater of the absurd consistently outdraws "thinky" political rhetoric. "At the end of the day, I think shows like that are just jealous of the ratings that wrestling's getting," he says. "I really wanted to say that on the show, but I didn't. I wish I had."

I ask Poffo about the appeal of the sport. Why does he like it? Why does anybody like it? "I don't want to be known as that old wrestler who knocks the young, because when we were young, the old guys knocked us. But I will tell you this, fans get sick of it and quit," he says, of wrestling. "And then you get new fans, and occasionally fans come back. I started out as a fan. I thought Johnny Valentine (father of Greg, The Hammer) was the greatest, and I couldn't begin to imitate him. Greg was good, but Johnny was better. Wrestling is a vicarious thrill. People don't support real wrestling in high schools, colleges, and the Olympics, but for some reason they pack arenas to watch this stuff."

****

Lanny Poffo is still writing poetry. He reports that he was recently invited back to Downers Grove, Illinois, where he recited a poem about the suburb, and counts among his greatest moments an invitation to Joe Robbie Stadium (Miami) in 1991 to recite a poem for Ted Williams. "As I was reading the poem, he started to cry," Poffo remembers. "He shook my hand afterward and said 'If I'd had you for a press agent, I would have never had any trouble.' "

Poffo is also pursuing acting and had recently returned from a trip to Brooklyn where, at his own expense, he auditioned for a role in the 2008 Darren Aronofsky film *The Wrestler*. Talk eventually turns back to the cruise, and Poffo is intrigued by the participatory wrestling angle of the book where I plan to train and then wrestle in a real match. "You know, you could wrestle me on the cruise," he says. "I would even put you over."

Chapter 3

Office Calls (Pain School)

There is something addictive and satisfying about getting nervous. It starts on the Monday before my first Wednesday class. I pack my gym bag—sweats, Under Armour, jock, socks—and begin to think about being the new guy. Walking in. Not knowing anyone. "It's hard core, man," was Jenig's last statement to me, on the phone, before I agreed to train with him. I roll that phrase around in my mind a few times. I know that everybody thinks their thing is the toughest—football players think they're the hardest core people around. Ditto for boxers and, apparently, pro wrestlers. It will be an experience.

I'm finding myself having to defend this book to my friends and family. "You're going to make it funny, right," they ask, hoping that this book will be primarily a satire of wrestling and its characters. Or they say things like, "At least it's a book deal," as though I just got a chapbook of 11 poems published by some outfit named Slippery Weasel Press and will receive 20 author copies in the mail for my efforts.

The more I think about it, the more I feel like wrestlers don't need justifying. If they want to put on spandex and grow hideous 80s mustaches and play fight, that seems like a perfectly normal and constructive thing to do. I guess I'm tired of sitting around discussing federal minimum wage laws, socialized health care, and Calvinism vs. Arminianism. More and more, I'm engaging in "boring intellectual talk," and I can see the handwriting on the wall, which is that people seldom have their minds changed and just like talking. Meanwhile, my body grows fat and pale, and I sit still in my office, waiting to be clever.

Still, I'm freaking out. I've brought along my cousin Brian for moral support, and we are a little late in arriving at the Pro Championship Wrestling Training Center, which is actually housed in Rick Jenig's garage, on Major Avenue in Chicago. My grandfather grew up a stone's throw from here, and the family used to own a restaurant[1] where I ate a huge prime rib sandwich for lunch, which I will probably regret about a half hour into the workout.

****

I got the call in November that my cousin Brian had fallen off the side of the Trump Tower in Chicago. He fell two stories off a ladder and was impaled through the thigh by a piece of re-bar. He was in the hospital in stable condition, with only, luckily, a chipped bone in his hip and a large, painful hole in his leg. It could have been much, much worse.

He was the reason I took this deal to begin with. Though our lives were very different as kids, wrestling was our one common bond. He subscribed to every wrestling magazine on the planet and has kept, it seems, all of them. We watched it together on Saturday mornings. We talked about it constantly. We saw our first live show together, at the Rosemont Horizon in Chicago, back when wrestlers and wrestling seemed larger than life. We built a ring in Gramps' backyard, made of matresses, a tarp, and garden hoses. Matches were filmed.

We both spent about 15 years not caring about wrestling, and, I suppose, we still don't care about it except for the nostalgia and the fact that it gives common ground. Wrestling is retarded, but it's escapism; and for that reason, it will always have value and a place in society. I just find it ironic that we trade DVDs that feature men falling long distances off ladders and through tables, and falling off a ladder is exactly what almost got him killed.

****

We're met by a tall guy in a black leather jacket who wears sunglasses, even though it's thoroughly overcast outside. He leads us through Jenig's backyard and into the garage, which is filled from wall

---

[1]Called The Old Barn, it was a popular Chicago speakeasy during Prohibition. According to family lore, the place played host to Charles Lindbergh, Ronald Reagan (when he was an actor), and the Chicago Bears on a regular basis.

to wall by a regulation wrestling ring. The tall guy is PL Myers, and we learn that the PL "can stand for several things, including "Promoter Large" and other things." It's also his first two initials. Myers is a PCW manager and "handles PR," and in the course of the first 10 minutes of our conversation, which includes a brief history of PCW, he drops the following names:

Bobby "The Brain" Heenan

Road Warrior Hawk

Road Warrior Animal

Jimmy "Superfly" Snuka

"The Heartbreak Kid" Shawn Michaels

Paul Ellering

Bret "Hitman" Hart

Kurt Angle

He also uses the phrase "keep the talent happy" and means it, not in an ironic or tongue-in-cheek way. We learn that Myers hosts a cable-access wrestling interview show in Chicago (*Wrestling Resource,* which won an award in addition to once covering a Mikhael Gorbachev press conference), and that he is frustrated by a glass ceiling of sorts that exists in the world of pro wrestling managers—a prejudice against tall managers.

"I'm 6′4′′," he says. "The Rock is 6′2′′, you're only 6′2′′, and that's the problem. Nobody wants to be walked into the ring by somebody that makes them look small. If ECW[2] was still around I'd definitely be in."

Myers, who has committed himself to paving the way for larger managers everywhere, has been rejected by Vince McMahon and the WWE but is undeterred, and has even kept his rejection letter as a memento. "Vince likes big guys," he explains, in what could be the understatement of a lifetime, considering all of the steroid allegations that have swirled around McMahon and his operation.

---

[2]ECW stands for Extreme Championship Wrestling and was clearly named back in the 1990s when the word "extreme," when attached to anything, was considered a marketing slam dunk. Seriously, ECW used to stand for East Coast Wrestling and was marked by its return to a hard-core (read: bloody), high-flying style of wrestling that utilized misfit characters (see: Mick Foley, formerly Cactus Jack) and made them superstars.

He often mentions "having lunch" or "having dinner" with (insert big-named wrestler). "It's (wrestling) like a sickness . . . it's like a rush of adrenaline for these guys," he says. "It's all about that 15 minutes of fame." On signing autographs: "That's why I'm in it. I'm in it to give back." He pauses for a moment. "I personalize all of them (autographs)," he explains, while I try to imagine Myers mobbed for autographs after a PCW show. "For 10 bucks, it's great family entertainment, and all of our guys sign autographs during the intermission. Seeing a kid's eyes get big and hearing him say 'That's PL Myers,' is what it's all about."

Myers switches easily from PR mode ("we've got the largest drawing promotion in the Chicago area") to self-promotion mode ("I've managed the Road Warriors three times"), to an introduction of the Ten Commandments of running a successful independent wrestling promotion.

"Commandment number one is 'don't depend on DVD sales to make a profit,' " he says, though we never get to commandments two through 10. Class is about to start, and I'm looking for a place to change. Myers motions me to the corner, where a small kerosene heater kicks out a bit of warmth. I wonder, for a moment, what the other homeowners on Major Avenue think when they hear the grunts, thuds, and other wrestling-related noises coming from this garage.

"Hey, we're Spartan here," Myers explains. "It's like *Rocky IV* . . . the one where he fights the Russian," referring to the scenes in which Rocky trained in a kibbutz in the middle of Russia, the commonality being that it was cold there, and it's freezing cold here.

****

After a fast, chilly wardrobe change, I leave Brian alone with Myers at ringside, for which I feel slightly guilty. Climbing through the ropes for the first time, I'm struck by how small the ring actually feels when one steps inside it. There are three other wrestlers in the ring, and it feels positively full. The mat itself is somewhat cushiony, but not exceedingly so, and it makes a satisfying, hollow thud whenever it is jumped or fallen upon. This is part of the show. The noise helps the wrestlers "sell" the pain.

A wrestler with six years of pro experience named Jay Phoenix leads the session. Phoenix was just named the PCW "Midwest" champion, continuing that great wrestling tradition of titles having geographical names with no actual geographical significance.[3] Phoenix, though, was an accomplished amateur wrestler and competitive shoot fighter[4] before settling on pro wrestling.

"I had a hard time transitioning from shoot fighting to fake fighting," he explains. "The first couple times I was in the wrestling ring I almost knocked guys out . . . I still wrestle stiff[5] but the difference now is that I'm safe."

Safety, thankfully, is a big deal at PCW. Phoenix assures me that I don't have to (and shouldn't) try any move that I'm not entirely comfortable with. Before any moves happen, however, Phoenix leads us through a calisthenics session that includes 50 pushups, 50 sit-ups, 50 jumping jacks,[6] 50 mountain-climbers, and a series of neck-strengthening bridge maneuvers in which you basically stand on your head and the balls of your feet and make a bridge with your torso, as the name would suggest.

This would be a good place to interject that I'm a fairly (emphasis on "fairly," because I'm a little fat now) fit 6′2″ and 225 pounds, but I am genuinely gassed after the warm-up routine. The other wrestlers in the class—both pros with two years of experience—are smaller, high-flyer types, while Phoenix, like myself, is more of a big plodder. He has cultivated a Canadian heel character, which makes sense in that he has a barrel chest, a big belly, and reddish-blonde coloring that one often associates with our neighbors to the north. He looks like he would be at home in a flannel shirt. When he isn't tumbling around a ring, Phoenix is finishing a degree in athletic training.

"I actually think it's harder to play the heel character," he explains. "As the heel, you control the pace of the match, but you're also

---

[3]Because the PCW has no region besides the Midwest, or more specifically, the greater Chicago area.

[4]Shoot fighting is, quite simply, real fighting. It's like the mixed martial arts stuff you seen on cable at all hours of the night, and it is growing in popularity. Chances are you know somebody or at least know somebody who knows somebody, who's training to be an MMA fighter.

[5]Wrestling stiff means that you come closer to actually hurting someone when performing the moves. Your punches may sometimes connect, and you squeeze harder when you have guys in holds. In general, the advantages to fighting stiff are that the matches look more real, but the main disadvantage, of course, is that you might really hurt someone.

[6]The noise generated by four 200-plus pounders jumping on the ring floor at once is almost deafening.

spending so much time making the crowd hate you that it can be distracting to focus on the guy across the ring from you. And then it's
your responsibility that you not only make the crowd hate you, but
you have to make them love the babyface."

After the warm-up, Phoenix leads us to a corner of the ring, where
we line up single-file and then run through a series of maneuvers:
two forward rolls, a leap over the ropes onto the ring apron and back,
a backward roll, a left shoulder roll, a right shoulder roll, and then a
back bump, which is perhaps the most foundational of all pro wrestling
maneuvers. The first wrestler is a compact Lucha libre[7] character
named "Fusion," whose real name is Jason. He wore a Lucha mask
out of his car and into the facility and seems to be in character throughout the proceedings. He zips through the drill with all of the stiffness
that one would exhibit while walking out to check the mail or bring
in the morning paper. He makes it look easy.

About halfway through the drill, I realize I haven't done a somer-
sault since Mr. Welge's gym class in grade school. The drill feels
rough, to say the least, but I get through it, even managing to land a
halfway-respectable back bump.

Next is a frat-boy type who goes by the ring moniker "Steve Heisman" and wears football pants and eye black into the ring. He is a
babyface character who is working on making the transition to heel.
He wears a "Fall Out Boy" T-shirt to training tonight, for which he
takes no small amount of ribbing, as Fall Out Boy is the obscure-
Chicago-pop-punk-band-made-good, which means they now suck.
Heisman looks like the type of guy you might run into at a North Side
bar, with his Cubs hat turned backwards and wearing a polo shirt and
khakis.

Heisman demonstrates each of the basic "bumps" for me—the back
bump, in which the wrestler falls directly backward onto the mat,
catching the brunt of the impact across his shoulder blades; the front
bump, in which the wrestler falls forward and takes most of the blow
on their forearms and thighs; the handstand bump, in which a handstand turns into a back bump; and finally the flip bump, which, as it

---

[7]*Lucha libre* is Spanish for "free fight" and refers to professional wrestling that takes place
in Mexico. Its stars are often athletic high-flyers, perhaps the best known of which is Rey
Mysterio Jr.

sounds, has the wrestler doing a front-flip and then landing on his back. It looks impossible—such that if I trained for the rest of my life, I probably couldn't pull it off.

"It took Steve a good four months to be able to do that," explains Phoenix, sensing my trepidation. "It's hard for big guys to train their bodies to go head over heels like that. Most guys our size have never done a flip of any kind—even into a pool."

After the bumps, we move on to rope running. Phoenix lets the more experienced wrestlers run through a long conditioning drill, involving one wrestler running the ropes from side to side while the other wrestler at times drops to the mat, at other times ducks clotheslines, and still at other times bends down so that the running man can leapfrog him. It's remarkable that neither man gets killed doing this sort of thing, and they actually make it look pretty good.

Phoenix lets me run the ropes myself. I'd been told that it's important to make contact with all three ropes at once, because to let your body hit only the top rope would be a good way to launch yourself over the rope and onto the arena (garage) floor. Periodically, he flops down in front of me, and I have to leap his prone figure on a dead run. Eventually, he sticks his arm out to simulate the clothesline that I would be ducking in a real match.

Running the ropes is exhausting, as is remembering the move combinations that wrestlers must mentally process through the course of a match. "With two experienced guys in there, you won't choreograph any of it beforehand," he explains. "You just do all of your communication in the ring, with only the outcome predetermined."

Fusion explains, through the Lucha mask, that he wrestled his first match after about six months of training, and choreographed the whole thing. "I want to work on my flippy-do stuff," he tells Heisman. The two men meet in the middle of the ring and perform a series of moves that involve Fusion launching himself off the ropes and head-scissoring Heisman, who then flips dramatically to the floor. They eventually bring a large "crash-pad" into the ring to attempt some edgier suplexes and other experimental moves. After each move, they ask each other, "you okay?" and then ask us, "did it look cool?"

While the two men work in the ring, Phoenix explains to me his aversion to maneuvers off the top rope. "I'm too big for those tricks,"

he says. "I'm more of a mat wrestler." He tells of a "moonsault"[8] inci-
dent gone wrong in which he "spiked it" a little bit on the landing. This
means he landed on his head. I ask him what it feels like on the top
rope, hoping that he'll invite me to try it. He does, and I do, wobbling
my way to the top rope, using his hand to steady me on my way up. My
head nearly touches the rafters at the top of the garage. My wobbly legs
launch me off the top rope, and I hit the mat with a satisfying thud.

****

The workout ends with some one-on-one chain wrestling instruction
from Phoenix. Chain wrestling is perhaps the most basic part of professional wrestling training, and may be the only part that has anything to
do with its ancestor—real wrestling. "I make my students keep a notebook and write down each move they learn each day," Phoenix
explains, as Steve Heisman produces a series of tattered notebooks.
"If I see something I like on a DVD, I'll write it down in here and bring
it to class."

The wrestlers themselves are a storehouse of information on the
sport, as they are all huge fans. Often during the lesson, they will reference a move they've seen on *WWE Smackdown,* or a DVD they
recently watched. Though it violates PL Myers's first commandment
of wrestling promotion, the DVD business has gone through the roof.[9]

Phoenix moves me through a series of maneuvers, beginning with
the "lockup," which is often the first move that happens in a conven-
tional one-on-one wrestling match. Phoenix eyes me from across
the ring, and I step at him, locking my left hand around his neck,
and placing my right arm on his left elbow. "You're like two great
warriors meeting in the center of the ring," he says. "Make it
dramatic, and move forward, keeping eye contact with your opponent." The ring thunders under our weight as the 250-pound Phoenix
and I lock up.

From there, I learn how to place Phoenix in a side headlock (make
sure the audience can see your opponent's face) and discover that the

---

[8]The moonsault is a move in which the wrestler stands on the top rope with his back to the
ring, and then performs a back flip, landing belly-down on his opponent, lying prone in the
ring. It's a way-cool move (made famous recently by the Heartbreak Kid Shawn Michaels)
but also a good way to get yourself killed. Moonsaults have been performed off of steel
cages, ladders, and scaffolding, in addition to the top rope.
[9]For example, WWE's *Great American Bash 2007* DVD moved 51,600 units and did over
a million dollars worth of business in its first *week* of release in August 2007.

side headlock is where much of a match's communicating takes place between wrestlers. The hammerlock (one arm wrenched behind the back) and the wristlock follow. And perhaps more importantly, I learn to "take" each of these moves. "A lot of guys will contort their faces in a move to try and 'sell' it," he says. "But it's really more important to act like you're trying to reverse the move or get out of it, because that's what you would be doing in a real fight."

I flop down on a folding chair at ringside after the workout, exhausted, but eager to write down what I'd learned in my own notebook, only to discover that PL Myers had stolen my pen.

****

Josh Abercrombie is laying face down on the ring mat when I enter the Price of Glory Wrestling School (Michigan Sports Camps) in Coldwater. There is an attractive young girl stroking his longish hair with one hand and with the other hand texting someone on her cell phone.

Via some e-mail correspondence, I learned that Abercrombie had broken his fibula in a match about a month ago, but has still been wrestling matches consistently since the injury in order to pay bills. He lifts his head when he hears me flop down on the ring apron. I ask him about the injury. "It sucks. It's not getting better." He pulls a sock down to reveal the puffy ankle that he wrestled on the night before in a Price of Glory[10] card billed as the "Murky Melee," in which he wrestled a character named Jack Thriller. "My bumps look a little funny now," he explains. "I've got to keep my right leg in the air."

I've decided to supplement my training in Chicago with the Price of Glory training—realizing that once or twice a month in Chicago wasn't going to cut it if I was to be match-ready by the end of the book. I swallow my pride and pay Mark Pennington the $95 per month in his tiny office and sign the Price of Glory contract ("and it is a contract"— his words) which assures him that I will pay $95 for the next four months. This was after giving it my best college try to attempt to get the training for free.

There are a handful of other newish students in the class as well—a skinny blonde kid from Grand Rapids (a two-hour drive from Coldwater), a kid from Detroit (a two-hour drive in the opposite direction),

---

[10]Price of Glory was named the "independent promotion of the year" two years in a row, according to manager/POG commissioner Mark Pennington.

and an older guy, Harley, age 63, who has been in the class for two years and has a tattoo of The Sheikh[11] on his left deltoid. It is an image of the Sheikh's head, with his trademark turban and the word "Sheikh" written below. I wonder for a minute if Harley is ever taken for a Taliban sympathizer due to the strange image of a random swarthy man in a turban on his arm. He strikes me as the type of guy who would otherwise be hyper-patriotic.

I learn from Harley that he fell off a ladder 25 years ago, when he was working as a mechanic, and broke his hip, his wrist, and his ribs and shredded every tendon in his shoulder. He found Price of Glory wrestling six years ago, shortly after undergoing open heart surgery. "I had a triple bypass," he explains, lifting his shirt to show me the scar, which runs from the top of his white belly to just below his Adam's apple. "I was struggling with the depression. I couldn't lift my left arm without using my right arm to help it up."

He walks me into the weight room, where little pencil markings run up the side of the white wall. These markings are a record of Harley's progress in lifting his left arm. He started on an ambitious weight training program then with Dan Severn and began attending the wrestling classes. He can now raise his arm above his shoulder without assistance. "I figured if I was going to die, I might as well die doing something I like," he says. His depression lifted, and he has been coming to the classes ever since. He's the school's longest-running student, and has, as he puts it "many illegitimate children" (the wrestlers).

"I was a little apprehensive about Harley starting the wrestling classes," says Severn. "I told him that if he died going through one of my classes that I was going to take his body down the street to Wal-Mart and put it in a shopping cart with a bottle of booze, and he gave me full permission to do so."

A youth Mixed Martial Arts[12] class is finishing up in the other portion of the gym. It's strange to see young kids (probably 8 or 9 years old) punching, choking, and chopping at dummies just like their favorite cage fighting stars. "This is the only youth MMA program in the

---

[11]Not to be confused with the WWE's "Iron Sheikh," who held the title before Hulk Hogan back in the early 1980s, this Sheikh is from Williamston, Michigan, where he ran a "territory" called Big Time Wrestling and was perhaps the first "hard-core" wrestler due to his affinity for things like barbed wire, fire, and heavy bleeding.

[12]Also known as the type of cage fighting you see on cable channels like Spike TV, which is packaged with gratuitous cheesecake shots and loud hip-hop music.

state," explains Mark Pennington, proudly. I certainly hope so. I think this but do not say it, knowing that in a few minutes I'll be flopping on the mat like a fish.

The back bump: Thrusting one's hips outward while falling backward to land on the fleshy part of the upper back. Legs in air. Slap the mat and exhale to emphasize the sound.

We do back bumps for what seems like forever. I'm going to feel this tomorrow. My forearms and hands, in particular, are smarting from hitting the mat time after time. I pause periodically to take in the scene around me—namely a handful of grown men randomly falling backward and hitting the ground. Grunting and slapping. This is weird.

The calisthenics (knee bends, running, shuffling, carioca, bridges, bridge pushups) winded me a little bit. I'm probably still about 15 pounds too heavy. And I'm seeing what a disadvantage height can be in back bumping. My 6 feet 2 inches feels like about 10 feet after a while.

The face bump: Much like it sounds. Drop elbows and torso down toward feet. Appear to land on face but actually land on forearms and upper thighs. Slap mat again. The key is to get thighs and forearms to hit the mat at the same time so that there is one thud and not two. Also, it's important to keep one's midsection off the mat so as not to rack oneself. "Save your dick," explains Abercrombie.

Perhaps the most exhausting part of this training is getting up off the mat after each bump. Fall. Get up. Fall. Get up. The pattern is endless and a little monotonous. After a while, the legs don't want to respond and pull the body off the mat, and it's against the rules to use your hands to get up. So we have to stand awkwardly by balancing on an elbow and a knee and then standing. I am drenched with sweat.

"Sometimes a guy will accidently come off the ropes and step on your hand," explains Harley.

"Or sometimes the guy is an asshole and does it on purpose," adds Abercrombie.

****

After mentioning something about more conditioning and more bumps, Abercrombie instead tells us to take a seat (thank God) and proceeds to tell us the Story of Wrestling.

"Okay kids, memorize this. It's amazing some schools don't teach this stuff before they let guys get into the ring in front of a crowd. The basic match has seven parts that, when followed, make it very hard to have a bad match.

"Wrestling is a story, just like a book—with an antagonist and . . . what do they call it . . . a protagonist?[13]" I nod in Abercrombie's direction, and he continues. "The story doesn't start in the ring; it starts when the wrestlers walk through the curtain. The heel always comes out first and he always starts doing heel stuff immediately—yelling at fans, refusing to slap five with kids, that sort of thing. You know right away that he's an asshole. Some guys just look like assholes." Abercrombie's respect for and excitement about the business of wrestling is apparent. He is not unlike a great college professor imparting knowledge to his students.

"Instead of a book, starting with something like 'My name is Ishmael' . . . " I cock an eyebrow. Abercrombie knows more about books than I thought. "A wrestling match starts with time to establish for the fans who is good and who is evil. In a book, the good guys do good stuff—help old ladies across the street, rescue cats from trees, and that sort of thing. In wrestling, the face might lock up and push the heel into the turnbuckle and then break cleanly. Then the heel might do the same thing and instead of breaking clean will slap the good guy in the face.

"The second part puts the babyface in control with a hold. The heel should call two or three high spots[14] for the babyface with the face ending up in the same hold he started with (arm drag, head lock takedown, etc.). When you start on a part of the body, always stay with it unless your opponent does something to injure another part of his body.

"In part three, the heel takes control by either heeling (hair, eyes, trunks, etc.) or catching the babyface out of a highspot. Or he could do something legal but vicious. And in this segment you'll work 2–3 highspots for the heel.

---

[13]Abercrombie is much smarter than he lets on, and I'm pretty sure he includes this, the pause, for effect.

[14]High spots refer to points in the match where the babyface performs big moves that put him in control and also work the crowd into a frenzy. A common mistake wrestlers make is to string a bunch of high spots together, rendering none of them actually "high," if that makes sense. It's got to be a tension/release sort of thing.

"The fourth part last about 15 seconds and involves the babyface starting a comeback but missing with something. Like he could go for a backdrop and get kicked, or run into a clothesline. The fifth part is when the heel starts getting nasty and tries to win using big moves followed by a cover. This is also the part of the match where the babyface almost wins with a desperation move (false finish). Don't use more than two false finishes for the babyface. Each time the face nearly wins, he must keep selling, and the heel should get madder and more vicious.

"Next is what the entire match is for—the babyface comeback. Ever been to a Jean Claude Van Damme movie? There's always a comeback. *Die Hard.* The good guy comes back. Everything we do in a match is set up for the comeback. It's the most important minute of the match—do it right and don't screw it up. In a proper comeback, the babyface is steaming mad, the heel backs off and the babyface corners him, and then the babyface attacks the heel and gives him three to four big moves.

"The finish starts the minute the comeback ends. Don't wait! After the comeback, go right to the finish. With Hogan it was always the same comeback and finish—he would reverse punches, whip the guy into the ropes, boot to the face, legdrop, and cover. Boom. Boom. Boom. Same thing every time, but very effective.

"But the biggest key, honestly, to getting over in wrestling is your look and your marketability. It's all about money. If you can make money for a promoter, then you're good for the business. John Cena[15] may not be the best wrestler in the WWE, but he is the most marketable. If you're 6-foot-6 and completely jacked, they don't even care if you can wrestle. They'll pay you 500 bucks a week plus lodging to train and develop. You can go out there and shit the place up every night, but if you look good they'll keep you around.

"If you want to keep getting booked, it's up to you to learn how to work a match and be able to do it. The wrestler who will learn how to work a match will be booked more and put over.[16] Those who can't will be booked less and do jobs.[17] You're doing more than just fake

---

[15]At press time, Cena was the WWE World Heavyweight Champion. He has acted in his own movie (*The Marine*) and put out his own rap album (surprisingly, not so bad).

[16]To be "put over" is to win. To get over with the crowd is to be well liked by them, and to put someone over is to both let them win and help them to look good while doing so.

[17]To "do the job" is to lose. Career losers are also known as "jobbers" or "jabronis."

fighting . . . people outside the business can't say 'fake' because it makes us mad . . . but we can say it. But to really work is to make something fake appear to be real. It's selling the lie. If I'm working a girl, I might tell her I have a 14-inch member."

Abercrombie stops his lecture for a moment and appears to be thinking through a college-entrance-exam cause-and-effect dilemma. "All my examples are sexual . . . one thing you'll learn is that wrestlers are sleazebags. All my friends talk like this, and all of my friends are wrestlers. I guess that means they're all sleazebags."

****

The morning after, my body is a festering mass of bruises and soreness. The insides of both forearms are bruised from repeatedly slapping the mat on each series of bumps. My neck hurts. However, I feel like I'm not really happy unless I'm getting my body beat up and feeling like this. What's wrong with me?

I've vowed to try and watch at least one wrestling match per day to try and better learn the craft, but I'm finding this difficult to do alone. One's enjoyment of wrestling, I've found, has a lot to do with who it is enjoyed with. When Vandermolen, Jarmo, and J. R. come over with a ladder match DVD, it's easy to get into the matches and enjoy the spectacle together. However, watching wrestling alone feels wasteful, somehow. I always feel as though there's something more productive I should be doing.

****

I'm driving Louis Kendrick home from another training session through an early-January Michigan snowstorm. Louis and I are car pooling from Lansing, as he has a leased car on which he "can't put over 800 miles a month." Kendrick drives close to 400 miles each weekend to wrestle in a promotion called EWF[18] in Marion, Indiana.

"They don't pay me anything," he says of the Marion promotion. Literally nothing, or just not very much? "Literally nothing. Not even gas." Kendrick is 22 years old, and a recent graduate of Michigan State University's prestigious telecommunications program. His parents are both professionals (a physical therapist and a schoolteacher) and, to say the least, are sweating his wrestling obsession.

---

[18]Note to all wrestling-promoter types: Can we put a moratorium on the word "extreme" for a while?

"They want me to focus on getting a real job," he says. "They think wrestling's a joke." For Kendrick, the options are look for a "career-type" job, or continue working hourly gigs (he has two) which offer more flexibility so that he can train and get booked at wrestling shows on the weekends. "I haven't gotten paid for a show yet," he explains. "That's how it is starting out, but this (wrestling) is bleeding me dry financially. I don't know if I can sell my soul to this like Josh (Abercrombie) has."

Earlier this evening, Abercrombie told the story in class, about the day that his grandfather died. A day in which he was in the car, a half-hour away from a booking, and he wrestled rather than going back home to be with his family. "You've got to be more committed to this than you are to your relationship," said Abercrombie. "Your character has to appeal to the broadest swath of the public. The best characters and the best angles relate to people—Vince McMahon and Stone Cold Steve Austin. Austin hates his boss. Who doesn't hate their boss? Ric Flair as the pampered rich kid. Who doesn't hate that guy? But then, who doesn't secretly, at least a little bit, want to be that guy? You want to be the guy who gets in the BMW and drives home from matches."

BMWs seem a long way from Abercrombie, Kendrick, and the rest of our class tonight. They appear to be fighting an uphill battle just to get bookings and, when they come, they don't pay or, at best, pay very little. Still, Abercrombie works tirelessly to get his students booked. Kendrick has worked each weekend for the last several months, often with another student named "Bri 2 Fly" who works a heel, boy-band angle in the ring.

Abercrombie also discussed the importance of working hurt. "If I break my ankle and I get replaced, I may never get that job back again," he explains. "So I wrestle hurt, rather than give up the booking that I worked so hard for."

We bumped tonight, but not as much as before, thank God. Kendrick and I both agreed that bumping on the cold, hard floor takes it out of you and is a bit much. It's much better bumping in the ring. Still, even doing 15 back, side, front, and face bumps felt like a lot and left me feeling weak for the remainder of the session, which included lots of chain work, which is fast becoming my favorite part of the practices. We learned the tie-up, wristlock, and waistlock tonight, and soon will be able to put two or three moves together.

In the car, Louis and I decide that the best characters are the ones that can combine serious wrestling talent with a gift for the irreverent. Basically, a tinge of humor needs to be added to any character, as wrestling is still essentially a circus-type environment. One of the most effective practitioners of this brand of humor was Rowdy Roddy Piper.

There's a video clip online from an outfit called All-Star Wrestling, that looks to be circa mid-seventies or early eighties, which shows Rowdy Roddy Piper (real name Roderick Toombs) smashing a real bottle of beer on his real forehead in a promo in order to generate excitement for an upcoming match. This program is hosted by the ubiquitous old white guy in a suit, and looks to be attended by about a hundred middle schoolers in their (probably) middle-school gymnasium.

Piper sounds very Canadian[19] in the clip, as opposed to later in his career when he donned a kilt and became the sort of caricaturish Scottish guy with a temper. Like Flair, Piper also got by largely without the help of an impressive physique, and has been notable since the beginning of his career, when he became the youngest professional wrestler in history at age 16. Since then, he has allegedly held 38 professional wrestling titles and has won over 7,000 professional wrestling matches including one against a WWF jobber named A. J. Petruzzi, in which he (Piper) wrestled with one hand behind his back, much to the delight of the Madison Square Garden crowd.

This match is typical of a Piper match from that era, in that Piper walked to the ring, accompanied by bagpipe music, chewing gum and looking either thoroughly bored or thoroughly intense. Even though Piper did lots of insane stuff (such as the beer bottle) he was often at his funniest/most entertaining when he was playing it straight, so to speak. Petruzzi, who was tall, fat and bearded in a Grizzly Adamsish sort of way, slapped Piper twice in the face to start the match. Piper then put the hand behind his back and kicked, chopped, and snap-mared Petruzzi with one hand, while still chewing the gum.

Piper started in the WWF as a heel, and remained so through Wrestlemania 2 in 1986, after which he had a leave of absence and returned, vs. Petruzzi, as a sort of de facto face, with the crowd chanting his name throughout the match. The zenith of this particular match came

---

[19]Piper was born in Saskatoon, Saskatchewan, and raised in Winnepeg, Manitoba. He has no connection to Scotland.

when Piper kneeled over a prone Petruzzi and slapped him several times on the face with his one (right) hand. Following the Petruzzi match, Piper feuded with Adrian Adonis, who I remember to be the first character with which the WWF experimented with sexual orientation. Adonis hosted an interview segment called "The Flower Shop" that Piper routinely crashed, leading to a Wrestlemania 3 hair match that in turn would supposedly lead to Piper's retirement to pursue his acting career.

To his credit, Piper did stay retired from wrestling from 1986 to sometime in 1989, making it longer than most wrestling retirements. To his credit again, he did actually make a few movies during this period, including *Hell Comes to Frogtown*, a B-cult film described as "conscious of its own unintentional hilarity" and *They Live*.

Piper's first WWF heel turn (1984–86) was highlighted by an interview show called "Piper's Pit," which featured Piper "interviewing" various other WWF personalities with whom he almost always ended up insulting and then fighting with later in the program. The "Pit" was held in a "studio" that looked like something your high school's drama department put together with plywood and paint in the back of the cafeteria, which somehow just added to the innocence and charm of the era. The set consisted of a tri-panel background featuring two large black-andwhite photos of Piper, and a large Scottish-looking crest, which is the part that looks like high school drama department construction.

The most notable "Pit" included an appearance by Samoan face high-flyer Jimmy "Superfly" Snuka, who was offered a pineapple (which Piper compared to the women of Samoa), a banana (later smashed in his face), and finally several coconuts in an attempt to "make Snuka feel comfortable" on set. "Piper's Pit" was entirely ad-libbed, and Piper's style seemed to involve talking loudly and fast in a delivery that didn't quite sound either Scottish or Canadian, but was definitely strident and not unfunny. Piper explained to Snuka that "the only thing I didn't get you was a tree to climb up and down like a monkey," which is, of course, horribly politically incorrect; but then again, this was the early 1980s, when people either had a sense of humor or didn't care, or both. And if you were watching the WWF on Saturday mornings in 1985, you probably weren't easily offended by such things. Piper then famously smashed Snuka in the face with a coconut that exploded satisfyingly on camera, and then sent Snuka careening into the aforementioned crappy set, sending the whole thing flying to the ground. Snuka was really hurt by this, of course, because coconuts are really hard and heavy and it would hurt to be smashed in the face with one. This, judgment in the heat of the moment was probably not Piper's strong suit. Piper then proceeded to smear Snuka's face with bananas, while at the same time calling him a "piece of junk." Another thing Piper routinely did, and also did in this particular "Pit," was to close one nostril and then blow the other nostril in the direction of his opponent. If you happened to be nine years old in 1985 (I was), you found this to be hilarious.

This is the type of behavior that allowed Piper to be named *Pro Wrestling Illustrated*'s Most Hated Wrestler of the Year, twice (1984, 1985) but also its Most Popular Wrestler (1986). Piper was an enigma. He claimed later in his career to hate his character, yet is a prisoner to it to a certain extent, as it is his means for making income. He also lost 75 percent of his hearing in one ear as a result of one of the dumber gimmick matches in wrestling history—a 1983 dog collar match against Greg "The Hammer" Valentine, which took place as a part of NWA's *Starrcade*.[20] Much like it sounds, the men were chained to each other via dog collars around each of their necks, making any move requiring more than a few feet of momentum impossible. The dog collar rendered rope-running null and void and resulted in what was, surprisingly, a pretty boring match considering the fact that it cost Piper much of his hearing. As was standard for most NWA matches of that era, it seemed dimly lit, bloody, and slightly depressing. Piper won the match by pinfall, using the dog chain for leverage.

When the WWE got "too serious" from the mid-1990s through the mid-2000s, they lost that ability to look at oneself in the mirror and laugh. Kendrick's character, then, is a wannabe kung-fu warrior—a black kid who idolizes kung-fu culture and tries to embody the moves in the ring.

Louis wrestled a "ring match" tonight—basically a 10-minute match as it would appear in a show. He was the babyface character and was wrestling another instructor named Brian who would get over. He

---

[20]*Starrcade* was the brainchild of Dusty Rhodes, who also booked (match-made) the event, and was the NWA's flagship event in much the same way that Wrestlemania was for the WWF/E. The first event was held in the Greensboro (North Carolina) Coliseum and drew over 14,000 fans, though only 30,000 or so, in total, watched on closed-circuit venues in the NWA's regular tour-stop cities.

captivated the small gym crowd and put on a great show, combining acrobatic maneuvers with solid mat wrestling. "That was probably the best match I've seen in this building that wasn't on a show," says Abercrombie who, to put it lightly, is sparing with praise.

Though Louis's parents worry about wrestling, and I don't blame them at all, they'll be glad to know that their son is a class act, a great conversationalist, and he wrestled a top-notch match tonight.

CHAPTER 4

Baron Von Raschke on the Claw, Ethnic Heeling, and Middle School Teaching

We've been married for 41 years, so we haven't known anything but wrestling. We learned about it together.

—Bonnie Raschke

The fact that Jim Raschke, heretofore referred to by his ring name Baron Von Raschke, taught middle school before becoming a professional wrestler may have given him a serious leg up on his competition. Though his physique was nothing special by today's "roided-up" standards, and you would never catch Raschke doing anything especially athletic—like a moonsault or a several-story dive through a table—he was perhaps the sport's most effective and even beloved heel. Nearly every man who spent any time as a young boy in Wisconsin, Minnesota, or Illinois in the 1960s and 1970s knows his name.

On his Web site, Baron Von Raschke.com, visitors can buy a "Claw powered" fishing lure, which speaks as much to Raschke's location in Minnesota as to his drawing power as a heel. The lure itself features a little rendering of Raschke, and a claw-shaped hook at the end.

Raschke was billed as a "dangerous German" and, in the late 1960s, took to wearing a red robe into the ring, where he would goose-step and generally look scary, sinister, and Eastern European. He was Ivan

Drago before Ivan Drago was Ivan Drago. There's really no way to describe his appearance other than to refer you to his photographs and YouTube clips. He was bald and funny-looking. He made funny faces. His promos were growly, raspy, and incoherent in much the same manner that made The Ultimate Warrior famous a decade or so later. So convincing was Raschke as a heel that it was common for fans to throw folding chairs and other objects at him on his way out of the arena.

There's something wholesome and innocent about Baron Von Raschke, age 68, and it may be the fact that his wife, Bonnie, answers when I call her home and promises to have her husband "awake and full of coffee" the next morning for our interview. In many ways, Raschke was fortunate to have heeled in an era before heels were expected to be truly deviant both in and out of the ring. It was before the twin dark clouds of recreational drugs and steroids truly made their mark on sports entertainment as well as real sports. Raschke was that rare heel who made an almost organic face transition later in his career. In his 1977 championship match with Bruno Sammartino, he was a hated heel; but by 1985, in another AWA turn, fans would cheer when he goose-stepped into the ring.

In fact, there is something wholesome about the entire 1970s and 1980s AWA scene. For the most part, the wrestlers seemed about as unroided up and normal as is possible for such a group of people. Broadcasts featured a then very noncontroversial Eric Bischoff, a less-roided Hulk Hogan, Bobby Heenan,[1] and Mean Gene Okerlund, who would all eventually make the jump to the WWF(E). Shows happened in places such as St. Paul, Kenosha, and Cheboygan, and generally wrestlers got over more because of superior ring psychology and less because of blood, ladders, tables, and seedy storylines. The rings were small, bouncy, and blue. For most of the AWA's existence, there were no valets. Of course, all good things have to come to an end, and during the AWA's death rattle it had a few ill-fated episodes on ESPN that were taped at the Tropicana in Las Vegas, and as is almost always the case in entertainment, nothing remains cool once it lands in Vegas.

"The business today has gone to the lowest common denominator," says Raschke. "It's all about shock value, and everything today is more

---

[1]Even then, Heenan was super talented and funny. For my money, this is one of the most entertaining personalities in wrestling.

blatant than it was back then. Back then, when there was a love scene, the oceans would roar and the rain would fall. People used their minds and their imagination. Now there are television shows that show the bullet going through the body, and then everyone standing there looking at the corpse. And in wrestling, they're showing their rears in the ring, and making love in the ring. It's low class. And you can tell Vince McMahon I said that."

Of course, McMahon did much more than just introduce lowbrow shock value into wrestling. He effectively killed the territory system in the early 1980s by buying up all of the territories' talent. So instead of kids in Texas growing up watching the Von Erichs on Saturday morning, kids in Georgia watching Ric Flair, and kids in Wisconsin growing up watching Baron Von Raschke and Verne Gagne, we're all left with whatever the WWE decides its demographic wants to see. This, I think, is what people are longing for when they talk about the "good old days" in wrestling. They want to identify with something germane to their region, rather than trying to choose which roided-up WWE freak to like.

It's only when one looks at Raschke and the old AWA that today's wrestling seems so, well, sad. The fact that Cactus Jack (Mick Foley) had to make a name by falling through rings and having appendages ripped off, and the fact that wrestling has made the crotch shot a part of American adolescent culture, seems especially sad in light of what wrestlers like Raschke were able to accomplish without such theatrics.

"We had ethnic heels and heroes back then, but we never slurred anyone's nationality," Raschke said, "and to be honest, I never remembered hearing a curse word."

****

Jim Raschke was born in Nebraska in 1940 and was that state's champion heavyweight high school wrestler in 1958. He then went to the University of Nebraska at Lincoln, where he wrestled collegiately and also made the football team, which was no small task. Raschke made the 1964 Olympic team as a wrestler, but an injured elbow forced him to sit out the games. He was teaching in a middle school and recovering from a knee injury when he discovered professional wrestling. "I had never thought much of it, but would watch it on Saturday mornings in the hospital lobby and finally realized 'I can do that.'"

Through a friend, Raschke was introduced to the dean of Midwestern wrestling, Verne Gagne, and went to Minnesota to train in Gagne's now legendary barn. "I borrowed my little brother's car to make the trip to Minnesota to meet with Gagne," Raschke remembers. "I learned after six weeks training with Verne that the endings were predetermined and that this was sports entertainment. But it doesn't matter who wins and loses in wrestling. The goal is to get people to come back next week. That's the crux of this business."

During the first months of his tenure with Gagne, Raschke's job was to set up the ring in a small, Minneapolis television studio, and then watch all of the matches from a control room, where he would peer out a window at wrestlers like Handsome Harley Race and Pretty Boy Larry Henig. "After a while I began to notice a short, hairy-looking guy who wasn't there during the week because he was always traveling. But he would stop at the door of the control room every week and holler 'you would[2] make a good German!' He did this week after week, until one week I shouted back, 'I am German!' I think I detected a bit of a smile."

The short, hairy man was, of course, Mad Dog Vachon, who would become Raschke's first regular professional wrestling partner. Still, the part of the Mad German didn't exactly come naturally. "One day Verne stopped by the control room and told me it was time to shoot an interview. At this time I was still Jimmy Raschke (pronounced rash-kee) from Nebrasky, so I mumbled and fumbled through an interview with Marty O'Neil, who was a really nice man. I was very shy and reserved then, and I've always been on the socially awkward side. When I finished, Verne came up to me and said 'Geez, that was terrible!' I was really hurt at the time, but he was right. It was a business to Verne, and he didn't want me hurting his business."

Raschke and Vachon bonded over their amateur wrestling history—Vachon was a Canadian Olympian—and soon he was packing a car and moving to Montreal, where he would debut the Baron Von Raschke character in earnest. "It was a natural for me because I had a squinty, snarly face anyway because I couldn't see," Raschke explains. "My German accent wasn't very good, but the fans in Montreal didn't care." The fans did, however, hate the big, bald, goose-stepping

---

[2]Raschke hollers this line into the telephone, and pronounces 'would' with a 'v' sound at the beginning.

German. "I couldn't see their faces because I was blind and wrestled without my glasses."

Without the advantage of seeing his audience, Raschke, perhaps more than other workers, was forced to gauge their reactions by hearing and feel. What he heard and felt was their boos, which is music to the ears of a heel. "My wife's former roommate sewed me a red cape, and the first time I interviewed in Montreal, I shouted 'I'm Baron Von Raschke!' and the words came out loudly and clearly. It's like I had tapped into an alter ego that had always been there."

Raschke went on to hold tag or individual titles in the AWA, NWA, and World Wrestling Alliance before his retirement from the ring in 1994. He wrestled extensively in Florida, Georgia, and Texas, as well as Michigan where he worked with The Sheikh.

"I was working for the Sheikh when I got a call from a promoter in St. Louis, where I was to work a show," he remembers. "They were paying for the match and transportation, so I traveled down to work with a guy named Pat O'Connor. In the middle of the match I had him in a headlock and he said 'put the claw on me.' I said 'What's that?' and he said 'Put your hand on my head.' Well I did, and the crowd went nuts."

The claw, it turns out, was the intellectual property of Fritz Von Erich, who was also working the territory at the same time. But Von Erich had given O'Connor carte blanche to use the claw at will, and it would soon become Raschke's calling card. It is also, perhaps, the simplest finishing maneuver in wrestling history, involving palming the other wrestler's head like a basketball while it is almost completely up to the other wrestler to "sell" what he's going through. Still, there is a bit of a philosophical discussion on how to best utilize the claw.

"Fritz used to slap the claw on right out of the blue, at any time during the match," Raschke remembers. "Whereas I liked to use it at the end and build the tension a little bit. It got to the point where if I didn't use the claw, crowds would be disappointed."

****

"My script, my script, my kingdom for a script! I'm looking all over the prop room for my script for the Baron! A play at the St. Paul History Theatre—spelled funny by the way. April fourteenth through May twentieth! The Baron is coming and he's not gonna be there to make fruit salad! He's there to act, in the best interests of all the people. And that is all you need to know!"

The above is from an ad that ran in St. Paul, which coincided with Raschke's acting debut in "The Baron," a play by Corey McCloud. In the ad, Raschke brandishes the claw and uses it to crush a piece of fruit—hence the fruit salad reference. I'm also fond of his plan to "act" in the best interest of the people. He was approached a few years ago by McCloud, a school-friend of his son Karl, and the budding playwright expressed interest in staging a play about the former wrestler. "I thought it was a school project," remembers Raschke. "I gave Cory a long interview, and then shared a bunch of press clippings and videos that people had sent in over the years. Initially I didn't know I would be acting in this play. I figured they would hire an actor . . . but I guess George Clooney wasn't available."

I ask Raschke if there were any similarities between controlling an audience in wrestling and what he experienced in theater. "Back in my day, wrestling was all ad-libbed so I didn't have any experience memorizing lines," he says. "I was terrified. When the play started out, it was total fear. The next night it was just a little dread, and finally, by the end, I was enjoying it."

The play traced Raschke's transformation from a Nebraska child to a world-famous wrestler. The production drew rave reviews, and was the subject of an article in the *New York Times*. "After the first night, the proprietor of the theater came up to me and said 'we've got a hit!' " he recalls. "I didn't know if the crowd reaction was good or not, because I wasn't used to theater crowds, but the other actors assured me that it was a good reaction. I didn't want to embarrass Heidi and Karl, but it went pretty well. We got over with the crowd.

"I always had a little different opinion of theater people," he says, honestly. "But they're nice. I went fishing with one of them just the other day. It was fun."

****

By the late 1980s the AWA was entering its twilight, and had a number of surreal television shows broadcast on ESPN. It was an odd confluence of sports and theatrics in to see wrestling's circus element on a network that takes itself and sports very seriously. The tapings took place in Las Vegas, Nevada, and by this time (1988) Raschke had grown a quintessentially 1980s mustache and had taken a face turn.

In a video featuring Raschke vs. a jobber named Pistol Pete, Raschke walks down the aisle to cheers, stopping often to high-five fans along the way. He is still billed as hailing from "the republic of Germany," as though the Baron was too large to identify with just one German city. Also, "the republic of Germany" seems much less sinister in 1988 than it did in 1967.

The Pistol Pete match was slow, but not unpleasantly so. It was sort of like playing nine holes on a crisp spring afternoon, or watching minor league baseball. It featured some slow hip tosses, a slow arm drag, and Raschke mugging for the crowd, who all love him. Raschke's body looks old and droopy because it is. He was 48 in 1988. I'm struck by the fact that in real life, we don't often see 48-year-old men shirtless, in tights. He performed a snap suplex, which Pistol Pete could have done a little bit more to help over.

Raschke slowly led Pistol Pete through a very loose match. He looked intent on not hurting his opponent, even when he bounced his head off the turnbuckle 10 times with the crowd counting along. Eventually, Raschke goose-stepped around the ring and used his left hand to grab his right wrist, signaling the oncoming claw. The television announcers were especially choice—Rod Trongard and Lee Marshall, undoubtedly two nameless,[3] faceless talking heads just getting their start on an ESPN ladder they would never climb, gambling wrongly that wrestling on a sports network would take off.

"There it is! He got it on tight!" says one, when Raschke applies the claw. "He puts it on so tight, Rod, his knuckles turn white! The master of his trade, here again, at the Showboat Sports Pavilion and Casino!" They seem less like ring announcers and more like sitcom actors parodying ring announcers, which, I realize, is actually more fun than real announcers.

In another 1988 ESPN match, Raschke faced a 270-pound body-building jobber named Daryl Nickle, who appeared to have been weaned on Anadrol 50. Looking huge and ripped, Nickle began raining blows on Raschke as soon as he entered the ring. Nickle then turned to pose to the crowd, giving Raschke time to recover. The announcer

---

[3]Rod Trongard, Lee Marshall. Trongard is actually something of a Minnesota sports legend, having called the Minneapolis Lakers, Minnesota Vikings, and Minneapolis North Stars in addition to University of Minnesota sports. Not even Trongard was immune to the siren song of the WWF(E) as he was lured there briefly in 1988.

chimes in, fantastically: "This is professional wrestling, and I think this kid is about to learn a lesson, Rod."

Raschke performed two arm drags and a backdrop, and then, again, began the goose step. The whole thing ended in three minutes and 15 seconds, and the announcers called it with every bit of enthusiasm one would expect for the main event at Wrestlemania. I realize that I miss these jobber matches. They are an afterthought now, a thing of the past. Most WWE television programming features filler (talk, storylines) leading up to a few key matches. In the 1980s, the jobber matches provided the filler, and it was much more fun to see what kind of stiffs[4] the promotions would come up with to serve as punching bags for their stars.

Even at his advanced age, Raschke also wrestled the occasional main event during this era, matching up with a very young Mr. Perfect, Curt Hennig, who was also from Minnesota's cradle of wrestling. Hennig was a perfect heel character, as he seemed to have been born with a cocky sneer on his face to go with a great physique and a better-than-average mullet[5] for the era.

This night, in 1988, the usually bored, jaded Vegas crowd is fired up at the thought of the old Raschke taking it to the new heel. Hennig billed himself as "Minnesota's Greatest Athlete," which seems odd, given that the match is happening in Las Vegas. Even Trongard and Marshall seemed to have an extra pep in their ringside call, exclaiming that the match is being broadcast "From coast to coast, continent to continent, and border to border." I imagine hungry, dirty South American children riveted to their televisions to see the outcome of this epic battle.

Like almost all heels, Hennig spent a lot of time outside the ring. Two teenage fans held up a sign that says "Curt the Jerk." According to the announcers, "these are the premier athletes in the world. Not only are they big and strong, they're fast. They can move like cats . . . they keep getting up time and time again when a lesser man or woman would be laying there completely out of it."

Raschke's match with Hennig was much stiffer than his previous work with the two jobbers and I'm impressed with the amount of

---

[4]Iron Mike Sharp, Barry Horowitz, Barry O, The Brooklyn Brawler. These guys were the A-list of jobbers, in my opinion.

[5]Hennig took advantage of the permed-mullet which was big at the time.

punishment his 48-year-old body could take. He took big backdrops and dropkicks in the ring. Meanwhile, the two announcers engaged in a long dialogue over Hennig's relative greatness when compared with other Minnesota sports legends like Bronco Nagurski, Verne Gagne, Jack Morris, Paul Molitor, and Kent Hrbek.

Wrestling was undergoing a paradigm shift in the late 1980s, and Raschke's involvement with the AWA was a prime example. He seemed to be the promotion's link to the past and nostalgia, while acts like the high-flying Midnight Rockers, a tag outfit featuring Marty Janetty and Shawn Michaels, were its future. In those days, the Rockers strode to the ring surrounded by fake security guards, to the strains of loud rock-and-roll music. Instead of black spandex, they wore ripped neon spandex, and their mullets were of the bleached-blonde variety. Girls screamed.

After a series of knife edge chops to his chest, Raschke began to stalk and sneer at Hennig, a signal that the claw is not far behind. He whipped Hennig into the ropes and applied the move, much to the delight of the crowd. While in the throes of the claw, Hennig accidently coldcocked the referee, who then rolled out of the ring and rang the bell, signaling a disqualification. Raschke then left the ring area to chants of his name.

****

These days, Raschke enjoys a quiet semi-retirement in Wabasha, Minnesota, which sits along the Wisconsin-Minnesota border and is known for its role in the *Grumpy Old Men* films as well as for good fishing. It seems an apt place for Raschke, who has been inducted into a couple of wrestling halls of fame[6] and enjoys local fame, if not riches.

"You know the show *Lifestyles of the Rich and Famous*?" he asks, rhetorically. "I forgot to get rich." I know it's a joke he's made often, but he seems truly at peace with his place in life. He expresses little regret after I ask him if there may have been another life for Jim Raschke that didn't involve playing an evil, claw-wielding German. He speaks fondly of his son Karl, his daughter Heidi, and his

---

[6]The Nebraska Scholastic Wrestling Coaches Association Hall of Fame, as well as the George Tragos/Lou Thesz Professional Wrestling Hall of Fame in Newton, Iowa.

grandchildren. His family life is astonishingly normal for someone in his profession.[7]

"It [wrestling] was okay with my kids," he says. "We moved around a lot, but we tried to move during good stages of development for them." Raschke makes light of the complaints of today's wrestlers, regarding travel. "Boo hoo," he says, "poor babies. They get to fly and take trains. We drove seven days a week. We drove from Minneapolis to Winnipeg and then back to Illinois to work the following night on two hours of sleep." Upon further reflection, though, he concedes that the travel changes are good for the sport. "I don't begrudge them flying," he says, "if it allows them to spend more time with their families. Being away from my wife and kids. That was the toughest part."

Raschke readily admits that the sport took a physical toll as well. He's had two knee replacements, wrist surgery, and operations on both shoulders. "But there are plenty of housewives and farmers who have had knee replacements," he says. "So I don't know if it was my profession or just life."

"I've always looked like this, so almost everywhere I go somebody recognizes me," says Raschke, when asked about fame now. "People always run down a list of wrestlers from their era, and just remember the good times they had. They always tell me that they used to sit on their grandpa's lap and watch me wrestle. It's just nice."

---

[7]Hulk Hogan, for example, seems to have become a walking parody of himself, appearing in a number of reality television shows including the train-wreckish *Hogan Knows Best*, which set new low standards for parenting. In June 2008, Hogan drew fire for a tape-recorded conversation he had with his son, who was serving a jail sentence, in which he discussed pitching his son's confinement as its own money-making reality show. Grim.

CHAPTER 5

Hulk Hogan (the Real American) as a Metaphor for Something

Rob Van Dam (Robert Alexander Szatkowski) is a professional wrestler from Battle Creek, Michigan, and also the star of RVDTV, whose distribution thus far seems limited to viewers at his Web site (Rob Van Dam.com) and whose content seems to include Rob Van Dam riding around in cars, doing flips into his pool, flexing, and talking with his "celebrity friends," none of whom I've actually heard of. Van Dam is something of a local legend here, due to his turn as WWE Intercontinental Champion and his experience with ECW. He has a real "Midwestern weightlifter" look about him, with the requisite ponytail, shaved on the sides. It's a very "Pantera in the mid 1990s" sort of look.

Van Dam's Web site also offers an opportunity to "explore your opinions on genuine conversations" as well as "insight to spiritual growth."[1] "I use adult language," says Van Dam in his RVDTV clip, "yet I consider myself a role model. That's not easy to explain in 10 words or less. That's why I've got my own show."

---

[1]Like a lot of other professional athletes, a number of wrestlers have expressed a desire to do more with their lives, in a spiritual sense, upon retirement from the ring. The Million Dollar Man Ted DiBiase is a speaker/evangelist, as is former NWA star Nikita Koloff, who now runs a Christian wrestling federation and gives evangelistic talks on the road. The problem with this, of course, is that people have made their living based on a charade and a willing suspension of disbelief, which in a way makes them the worst possible people to argue for belief in something.

Having your own show in this day and age is, of course, relative. If having streaming video of yourself available on your Web site is what having a show entails, then lots of people "have a show." Van Dam's Wikipedia entry also promises "an upcoming DVD on stretching" which will no doubt prove to be scintillating.

Van Dam, to steal a line from Isaac Hayes, is a complicated man. The road to wrestling success is often paved with something as simple as a memorable catchphrase or signature move. Witness Hulk Hogan "Hulking Up" and ripping T-shirts—simple but memorable. Van Dam's move is equally simple. It's Van Dam, like many of my five-year-old son's friends, saying his name—"I'm Rob. Van. Dam"— while at the same time flexing his biceps and pointing with his thumbs, at his face. Go to the mirror and try it, except substitute your name for Rob's. It's fun. But for being such a big guy, at 5′11″ and 237 pounds, Van Dam was a pretty unbelievable high flyer, and could often be seen doing flips off the ropes, and out of the ring, that were previously the territory of much smaller guys.

I mention Van Dam in the context of Hulk Hogan only to illustrate that wrestling stardom is not as easy and formulaic as it seems. At first glance, the most boring Rob Van Dam match is infinitely more exciting, athletically speaking, than the most heavily hyped Hogan match. Simply put, Hogan's matches were, from an acrobatic standpoint, pretty boring, and were rarely, bell to bell, over eight minutes long. So why is it that the acrobatic Van Dam, with an honest-to-goodness shoot fighting background pre-wrestling, will be largely forgotten, while Hogan endures? Call it charisma, or lack thereof, or ring politics. Or perhaps it was the fact that Hogan wrestled in an era of clearly defined good guys and bad guys, whereas Van Dam's era was more nebulous in this area. At any rate, Van Dam is temporarily retired (maybe permanently), and said this in an early 2008 interview with the *Baltimore Sun*:

It's been just business for me for a long time. The passion got burned out a long time ago. Keeping up with it, watching it on TV would be like you watching other people work in a cubicle. That's really what it felt like. I started looking at the crowd and I would say, "What are these people doing here? They watch this every week on TV, the same guys, and most of them don't even try to be creative. They just try to be like someone they liked growing up and they steal everyone else's moves." And I'd look at the crowd and I'd say, "Why? Why do these people leave their homes to come out and see this?" That's how burned out I was, and that's when I knew I needed a break.

What Van Dam describes is the selfsame feeling that most American working folks experience every morning on their way into work, and it is exactly that feeling that they go to wrestling shows to try to escape. What Van Dam verbalizes is, in fact, a very dangerous sentiment. Many heels have made a career out of pretending to disrespect the audience, and what Van Dam, in a moment of very real and in many ways winsome honesty, has done is to disrespect the audience for real. It's something Hogan never would have done. In a sense, Hogan's complete inability to be ironic or even honest was his single greatest quality.

The tagline on Van Dam's Web site is "Imitated often.[2] Intimidated never!" which, grammatically, strikes me as a little awkward. I would have gone with "often imitated, never intimidated," though neither would be true in my case.

****

It was almost a foregone conclusion, shortly after I decided to write this book, that I wouldn't get a one-on-one interview with Hulk Hogan. E-mails to his Web site went unreturned. Ditto for messages left with a network publicist working with Hogan on *American Gladiators*. Somebody once asked me to fax in a request, which I did, but the request is publicist talk for "screw off; you're never getting the interview."

In many ways, Hogan is breathing his last as an American public figure. His reality television shows have become more and more pitiable, and soon, rather than carrying his own reality show, he will merely be a guest on one, and then disappear altogether. Currently he is the host of *Gladiators*, a rehash of a show that was popular in the mid-1990s. The show is entertaining, as it features super-athletic regular people, usually firefighters, National Guardsmen, or high school coaches, squaring off in athletic events against huge, ripped über-athletes with names like Rocket, Jet, Titan, Venom, and Wolf. These über-athletes all wear colorful spandex, while Hogan usually sports a black spandex cutoff shirt, and a black bandanna to cover his balding dome. The show

---

[2] I haven't encountered many Van Dam imitators, but I suppose it's possible.

is really a celebration of youth, virility, and athletic achievement, which makes an aging Hogan really the only incongruous choice on the program. He announces events in his gravelly baritone, and says "brother" a lot.

My first recollections of Hogan begin with his WWF(E) title reign, starting with a stirring victory over the Iron Sheikh back when it was okay to be an ethnic heel, and Hogan was a real American, fighting for the rights of every man. The song Hogan had played when he entered the ring is now burned into my mind forever. It went something like, "When it comes crashing down and it hurts inside, you gotta take a stand it won't help to hide. When you hurt my friends, then you hurt my pride, I've gotta be a man, I can't let it slide. I am a real American, fight for the rights of every man. I am a real American. Fight for what's right. Fight for your life." To my knowledge, Hogan has never actually fought for the rights of any man, but it was nevertheless a catchy and effective jingle, and one he used well during a wrestling era during which you were either a real American[3] or you were, horror of horrors, foreign.

Hogan's body, in many ways, is a testament to American medicine and resilience. If nothing else, he's proof that you can bleach your hair, shave your chest, and fake-tan your entire life and still, well, be alive. He has crushed vertebrae, torn muscles, ruined knees, and broken ribs, all in the name of wrestling, and on television seems none the worse for wear.

On April 29, 1985, Hulk Hogan (real name Terry Bollea) appeared on the cover of *Sports Illustrated* magazine—the same magazine that published John Updike, George Plimpton, Norman Mailer, and Frank DeFord, among other literary elites. It was, in many ways, as close as wrestling would get, in the modern era, to actual legitimacy. There was a time when Hulk Hogan couldn't walk down the streets of New York City without being mobbed. This was all yet another example of the kind of creative synergy dreamed up by Vince McMahon, who has been many things, but is nothing if not a wellspring of ideas. McMahon's idea was pretty simple—to get real people in pop culture to legitimize pro wrestling and the WWF(E) by being interested in it. He paired Hulk Hogan with Mr. T in a *Wrestlemania* tag match, co-opting Mr. T's television celebrity as B. A. Baracus on *The A-Team*.

---

[3]Like Hacksaw Jim Duggan and Sgt. Slaughter.

McMahon used pop-music star Cyndi Lauper as a cog in various story-lines. No less than Muhammad Ali, Liberace, Billy Martin, Bob Uecker, William "Refrigerator" Perry, and Mary Hart (among others) played large roles in *Wrestlemania*s 1–3.

Nothing is inherently significant about celebrity appearances, but these appearances were significant in that they didn't seem in any way ironic or tongue-in-cheek. There was no eye-rolling. It was as though these celebrities viewed wrestling as somehow worth their time and attention, which just further validated it for the rest of us. At risk of stating the obvious, this doesn't happen much anymore.

Hogan was at the center of this energy, and stood in stark contrast to the WWF's previously significant champion, Bob Backlund. As Leave-it-to-Beaverish and clean-cut as Backlund was, Hogan was equally surferish and cool. And he was huge, at 6′9′′. Real wrestling critics (I'm not one, obviously) will argue that Hogan couldn't wrestle, but does it really matter? In much the same way as Baron Von Raschke, Hogan was a master of ring psychology back when ring psychology mattered. He succeeded in doing what John Cena succeeds in doing now, and that is, primarily, making you want to watch him. Hogan's emotions in the ring seemed to ebb and flow with those of the crowd, and he made standard things like ripping off your shirt in the ring, or cupping a hand to your ear to hear the applause of the crowd. Hogan's star began to rise with an appearance in *Rocky III* (1982) opposite Sylvester Stallone. He essentially played himself in the film, appearing as a brash, arrogant, but ultimately good wrestler named Thunderlips, who smacks Stallone around in a celebrity wrestling match.

The Thunderlips part led to additional Hollywood turns in really unfortunate movies like *No Holds Barred* (1989) and *Mr. Nanny* (1993), as well as a bad *Miami Vice* television knockoff called *Thunder in Paradise*. The fact that these movies and shows were unwatchable isn't as important, though, as the fact that they existed at all. Hogan's existence in Hollywood[4] proved a certain mainstream acceptance of wrestling at the time, and paved the way for future wrestlers-

---

[4]Perhaps Hogan's best contribution to pop-culture was the CBS Saturday morning cartoon called *Hulk Hogan's Rock-n-Wrestling* which featured good guys like Hogan and the Junkyard Dog solving mysteries and foiling the sinister plans of heels like The Iron Sheikh and Nikolai Volkoff. The show was proof of the mainstream success of wrestling, and the fact that wrestling was, at that time, clean and wholesome enough for kids.

turned-actors like The Rock to make movies that are infinitely better and almost watchable.

Given that you are reading this book, you can probably recite Hogan's in-ring history more thoroughly than I can. You know that on his first day as a wrestling trainee, he had his leg broken (on purpose) by Hiro Matsuda. You know that for a while, his ring names were the very porn-ish Sterling Golden and later Terry Boulder. You know that he actually ended his first stint with the WWF(E) in 1980 and joined the AWA in 1981. You know that he sort of won AWA titles in 1983 in a series of screw-job finishes with the ancient Nick Bockwinkel, who was a favorite of promoter Verne Gagne. You know that Gagne wanted the title to reside with wrestlers who were "old school" and could actually wrestle, even though Hogan was far and away the AWA's most popular commodity. In a dispute, in part, over percentages of merchandise sales, Hogan would leave the AWA in 1983 and start his second WWF(E) turn. The rest is, of course, history.[5]

It's easy to wonder why the AWA title, or any title for that matter, means anything in a sport that's, well, fake. In a way, it doesn't mean anything, in the same way that Matt Damon playing a super-powered spy in the Bourne movie trilogy doesn't mean Matt Damon is actually a super-powered spy. It does, however, mean advancement in one's career, which is why wrestlers express true (not staged) excitement over winning title belts.

But Hogan's salesmanship of this excitement both in and out of the ring was, I think, the key to his success. When Hogan flipped out after winning a title, and went to each corner of the ring to play to the crowd, it made you (the fan) excited. It helped to be nine years old, but it was still captivating and exciting to see. In Hogan, there was no sense of irony or cynicism in his frenzied celebrations, just good old American dream-following and prosperity. It comes as no surprise that he was incredibly popular.

Hogan followed a long title run in the WWF(E) with a heel run in the now-defunct WCW in which he donned black gear and wrestled as a sort of money-grubbing "Hollywood" icon, which, ironically, may be more true now than ever. In WCW, Hogan began to seem pathetic

---

[5]A long title run with WWF(E), an unfortunate (to me) turn in WCW in which he turned heel for a while and work black into the ring instead of red and yellow and seemed to age decades at a time, and then another turn with WWF(E).

and old; and, at the risk of sounding sentimental, it was strange to see him wrestling in anything other than red and yellow.

In many ways, Hogan is, now with the family crisis (divorce, parenting issues), more of a "real American" than he's ever been before. If surveys, polls, and statistics are to be believed, America struggles a great deal with these issues. America also loves to see celebrities dismantled and destroyed.

Chapter 6

Meeting a Real, Live Diva: Pro Championship Wrestling's Winter Meltdown and ``Sunny´´ Sytch

This is like the circus, except there's no performers and it's all carnies.
—Brian Erickson, Fan

The thermometer in my car says it's three degrees outside the Don Preston Community Center in Midlothian, Illinois. A handwritten cardboard sign stuck into the frozen earth in front of the center reads "PCW Wrestling Tonight 7 PM." It's the kind of sign that might usually say "For Sale by Owner."

The Preston Center looks like a grade school from the outside. There is an assortment of playground equipment outside, and inside is a gray gymnasium and a door labeled "Senior's Corner," where older folks gather to play checkers when the room isn't being occupied by grown men dressing in spandex.

We're welcomed into the gym by a man in his mid-sixties wearing a shirt that says "Hot Bod Shawn Davis" and a younger girl who explains that "my fiancée is Whiplash." Whiplash, I learn, is 33 years old. She points him out, and he's one of a number of very ordinary guys putting the ring together in the center of the gym. I consider asking her how long "Whiplash" has been wrestling, but I feel silly saying "Whiplash" to Whiplash's fiancée as though his name is real.

Rick Jenig, whom I've never met in person, is walking around the gym barking orders at the guys putting the ring together. They're all wrestlers on tonight's card, and it's clear that Jenig is the ringleader in this circus. He approaches a short, swarthy wrestler named "Uzi" (the Hebrew Hammer) who is chatting on his cell phone. "What are you doing?" Jenig asks. "Nothing," replies the Hebrew Hammer. "Exactly," says Jenig. Uzi slinks back toward the ring, which is now just a pile of steel, plywood, and padding.

"They're guys," Jenig explains. "If you don't yell at them, they won't do anything." Jenig stands about 6´3´´ and wears glasses. He isn't what I expected, and is probably the only guy in this room who doesn't look like he worked in the audio-visual room in high school, or spends a lot of his time in comic book shops. I'm struck that his oddly effective management skills could probably be much more lucratively utilized in other areas. He conducts himself not unlike a successful coach. He's mean, but everyone seems to like him and respond.

"This crew is just as passionate as the guys setting up for the Super Bowl," my dad says, as we watch the show come together around us. This is by far the weirdest thing he has ever attended. The lobby is filling up with fans, here more than two hours early. Lots of black T-shirts, pale skin, bad hygiene. I spot a GWAR t-shirt. "These are the people that society forgot," my dad remarks. "They fell through the cracks and ended up here." He's getting philosophical already, which I think may be the only way to get through something like this.

"Are those fog machines full?" Jenig is shouting to nobody in particular now, as the time to open the doors is only minutes away. "We need to get the lights synced up with the music," he explains. "I can't have Whiplash walking out to Steve Heisman's music. And where's the Butcher?!?"

****

PL Myers, the tall manager, walks through the locker room (Senior's Corner) doors a little after 6:00 p.m., with former WWE diva Tammy Lynn "Sunny" Sytch in tow. Meyers is dressed in event garb, which for him is a three-piece suit, an English-style driving cap turned backwards, and a cane with an eight-ball on top. His pants are a good inch or three too short.

Sytch is immediately situated in front of a giant background fashioned from blue construction paper and Scotch tape, where she'll have her picture taken for the next 40 minutes in a variety of increasingly smaller outfits. She goes to the dressing room (an activities office in the rear of the center) to change and then comes out to primp in front of a tiny mirror that falls off the wall two or three times during the course of the shoot. She looks like she's spent a good part of her life getting her picture taken by dirty-old-man types. Purse lips. Turn shoulders. Seductive smile. Change clothes. Click. Repeat. I wonder what will become of the hundreds of photos that are taken here. She implores the photographers to take only pictures that portray her above midwaist, because she thinks she's getting fat (she isn't). The photographers, to coin a well-worn cliché, are just happy to be there. The construction paper is bordered by a handmade poster that says "December Birthdays" and a taped-up "ABCs" primer intended for kindergartners who probably use this room as a day-care center during the week.

The opening bell is fast approaching, and the wrestlers who have dressed in a large common area are milling around and preparing in their own way. "Hot Bod" Shawn Davis—the youngest-looking wrestler in the promotion, and perhaps the only one with a body that I would characterize as "athletic"—picks up a set of dumbbells to get a pre-match "pump." Davis, according to the sheet of notebook paper tacked to the wall, is scheduled to win the PCW Chicago Championship tonight from Jay Phoenix, who trained me a month or so ago. He'll also appear in a "Royal Rumble," which will determine who will face Aries in a "world" title match at the upcoming Dream Night event.

Davis and a supposedly French heel character named Jean-Paul Bassey both work at an animal hospital when they're not wrestling. This was after Davis tried, unsuccessfully, to convince me that he was a "male gigolo" in order to keep up the appearances of his character. They've both been at it for about a year, and were roped into the business by Uzi. We're joined by The Butcher, who arrives late with an older man named Rodney, who describes himself as The Butcher's agent. The Butcher is about my age (31) and looks like he just stepped off the back of a Harley. Long, stringy hair. Jeans. Leather jacket. He will remove the leather jacket and wrestle in the rest of his outfit, which includes a white T-shirt dappled in dried blood from previous matches. His forehead is laced with scar tissue arranged in perfectly straight lines, which means that The Butcher is known for blading himself and then bleeding all over the place. This, according to Rodney, makes the crowds go crazy.

"His mom told me once that wrestling was the best thing that's ever happened to that kid," says Rodney of The Butcher, who is outside smoking a cigarette. I learn that he (Butcher) has been in and out of prisons around the area for most of his adult life, though he seems to be a popular figure among the other workers. Rodney explains that they are working together to try to expose him to TNA (Total Nonstop Action),[1] but that money is tight and promo videos are expensive. Time seems to be running out on The Butcher. I ask Rodney what his wrestler does in real life. "He's a butcher," he replies. This may or may not be true, but I'd like to believe that it is.

In the center of the room, "The Party Animal" Wally Wylde, a wrestler and business associate of Jenig, is giving the final pep talk. Wylde wears blue shorts, a "Party Animal" T-shirt, and luau-style leis into the ring. "They've got standing room only out there boys," he says (cheers). "This is a chance to play the crowd and put our best foot forward. This is a big show . . . just remember to do play the crowd!" The boys gather around Wylde and put their fists in the air. "PCW on three. One. Two. Three. PCW!"

****

The matches are a blur. It's a dark room, and there's a succession of spandex-clad people in and out of the ring. Lots of loud music. Lots of different people shouting things into microphones. Just an odd cacophony of disjointed noise. Jean-Paul Bassey and Uzi (the Foreign Connection) lose their tag match, and the highlight includes someone breaking a loaf of French bread (true story) over Bassey's head. Jared Priest (big, shaven head, goatee) beats a character named "Sacrifice" who looks to be some sort of postmodern Christ-figure (skinny, dark, long hair, beard, jeans). Sacrifice is kicked in the head so hard during the match that the sound resonates out into the seats. He will later be taken to the emergency room by Rick Jenig, who will miss the rest of the show, including Sunny's spot with PL Myers.

---

[1]TNA is the "other" big-time wrestling promotion on television. Their shows are broadcast on Spike TV, and they are struggling to compete with the much larger WWE.

In said spot, Sunny is paraded out in front of the leering crowd, and she sets up a storyline which she does in every tank town she visits. She incites the local manager (Meyers) and agrees to find a "suitable man backstage" (Hot Bod Shawn Davis) to wrestle the local manager's heel (Jay Phoenix). The losing manager has to kiss the feet of the winning manager. She recites lines like "find a suitable man" as though she's said them many times before. Not quite bored, because she is a professional, but also not entirely interested. She recites these lines and then retreats into the activities office/dressing room until she's needed to sign autographs during intermission.

Behind us, a drunk fan[2] has been shouting the vilest of sexual insults at Sytch and the rest of the wrestlers, both male and female. It's a disgusting display and embarrassing to everyone in our section which includes a number of young kids. As if reading my mind, my dad says, "That guy isn't worth the damage it would do to your hands."

****

Getting the interview with Sytch is proving (not surprisingly) to be a little more difficult than I had planned. I've taken up residence in the dressing room, right by the door that leads to the ring. Often I'm there alone, but occasionally a wrestler will walk up for a chat. Truthfully, I enjoy the atmosphere more back here than I do out in the gym. It's quieter, and not at all crazy.

"Why are you standing over here all isolated?" The question comes from "December"—a girl wrestler dressed in a black-and-white cheerleading uniform and wearing pigtails. "I don't want to get in anyone's way," I tell her. She proceeds to tell me that pro wrestlers are, like, "the best people ever . . . better than teachers." I also learn that she is an English undergrad student and hopes to teach high school English someday. Her favorite poet is Robert Frost. She thinks Carl Sandburg is overrated. Her colleagues don't know she wrestles, and her parents didn't for a long time, until a friend let the cat out of the bag. They were less than pleased. She will take part in a "Royal Rumble" tonight, where she will be spanked and then thrown out of the ring. Score one for women's rights.

---

[2]Note to that drunk fan: If, by chance, you're reading this (which assumes literacy—not a given), you really need to get help.

"Have you seen Sunny?" I ask her, wondering if perhaps Sunny pulled her aside to share some girl-on-girl wisdom from the road. She hadn't, and December just points to the door to the activities office. My interview was supposed to happen after the photographs and before the show, but has already been put off once. I swallow hard and knock. "I'm on an important call," says Sunny, swiveling out of a cubicle where, if this wasn't Saturday night, and she wasn't a diva, she could have been planning the schedule for Midlothian youth basketball leagues or senior's cribbage. "Come back after the intermission."

The match before intermission provides by far the best entertainment of the night and features the Davis/Phoenix/Sunny storyline. Sunny accompanies young Davis into the ring, though they've barely spoken backstage, and she does a fine job of getting the crowd excited about him. Later, the cartoonish Meyers stalks out of the dressing room with Phoenix in tow. A good 50 percent of the time spent at a professional wrestling show is spent not watching any actual wrestling. The ring walks, the pre-match posturing that happens inside and outside the ring, and the usually pointless shouting and taunting that happens before the match take up the bulk of the time. There's a fine line between playing the crowd, and wasting the time of the crowd.

But like any good manager, Sunny walks the fine line between adding value to the match, and distracting the crowd from the action in the ring. In this case, the action is significant. Phoenix, though a large wrestler, hits several high spots during the match, culminating in a suplex off the top rope, which sends him and the much smaller Davis crashing into the mat. Davis rallies and proceeds to hit three huge elbow drops off the top rope—his small body soaring through the air until he crashes onto the mat near (not on) the prone Phoenix. He is presented with the strap (wrestling parlance for title belt) after the match and, as per her storyline, Sunny forces PL Myers to kiss not hers, but Shawn Davis's feet.

****

The house lights go on, and Sunny is sequestered in a corner of the gymnasium where she will sign autographs for the better part of an hour. Her customers include dirty old men, teenage boys, small children, and prepubescent girls dressed in too little clothing and too much makeup. I begin to wonder how she handles this emotionally.

Post intermission is the "Royal Rumble"[3] to determine who will face the reigning PCW champion. Oddly, the event starts when most of the fans are still milling around getting refreshments or trying to glimpse Sunny, and it also features the running commentary of one of the wrestlers who has grabbed the microphone. I keep one eye on the line in front of Sunny's table, and one eye on the clock, glancing occasionally at the action in the ring. I can see my interview slipping away.

I hastily walk back to the locker room to stake out a section of wall, so that I can catch the eye of Meyers and Sunny as they make their way back to the dressing area. The Rumble finally ends (winner: Party Animal Wally Wylde) and Sunny presses through the mass of humanity with Meyers running interference. Oddly, the picture Meyers painted of him signing autographs for adoring children actually comes true, and I feel a little sheepish for having doubted him. They are adoring children, and they are, oddly, asking for his autograph. Meyers catches my eye and waves me back into the activities office, where Sunny sits with one of the photographers hovering close by. On my way to the office, I pass by The Butcher, who once again bladed himself to give the fans the blood that they like to see. He looks spent, and is sitting on the piece of construction paper that once served as Sunny's background. His forehead is bleeding profusely, and little droplets of blood indicate his path through the dressing room, and to this spot.

****

Sunny doesn't look up from a small compact mirror when I enter the room, but she will go from jaded and bored to engaging and friendly over the course of the next few minutes. "I do this every single weekend," she explains. "Every Friday, Saturday, and Sunday." She sounds a little exhausted but goes on to explain that she's not exactly cut out for the daily grind of nine-to-five work. "Could you imagine me in a nine-to-five job?" she asks, rhetorically. "I'm not a nine-to-five type of girl." I tell her that I certainly cannot, though I'm lying a bit because I don't know a lot about her, and we've just met.

---

[3]This format features two wrestlers in the ring, with additional wrestlers added every couple of minutes or so. The idea is to throw your opponents over the top rope and out of the ring. This results in their being out of the competition. But it's confusing, because wrestlers are entering and leaving the ring all the time, so there's always somebody walking around outside the ring, and you never really know who's in and who's out. This works better on television.

I ask Sytch about fame, and if it is as tedious as it seemed tonight in Midlothian. "How can you get tired of fame?" she asks, again, rhetorically, as though getting tired of fame might just be the craziest idea she's ever heard. She laughs, and her laughter indicates equal parts New Jersey, cigarettes, and fatigue. Her theology of fame seems to be that fame is the End Game. It's the pot of gold at the end of the rainbow. If one has fame—people asking for autographs, even in Midlothian—then everything else falls into place. Her reading of a place seems to be directly dependent upon how she is received.

"I absolutely loved Japan," she says. "I would walk down the street in Tokyo and people would just chase me down the street like I was Marilyn Monroe. You can get the Japanese to do anything for you. I came out of my hotel room at four in the morning once to get some ice, and there were four Japanese guys waiting in the hallway just to see me."[4]

I ask her if it's more difficult here, in small venues, to connect with the crowd. "It's actually a lot easier," she says, warming a bit. "You're more personal with the crowds at a place like this. You can look them in the eye so they don't have the option of being bored or looking at something else. They can't look away from you."

Sytch is a girl from Matawan, New Jersey (born 1972), whose career has taken her from Tennessee (more on that later) and an outfit called Smoky Mountain Wrestling to the WWE and trips around the world. In Smoky Mountain, she played a character who supposedly went to Wellesley and idolized Hillary Clinton. She was hated, and managed her real-life high school sweetheart, Chris Candido, who would accompany her to the WWE in 1993. Her career hit its apex in 1996 when she won two Slammy Awards[5] in 1996, for "best buns" and "best manager." Released by the WWE in 1998, she would make short stints in both ECW and WCW before hitting the independent circuit semi-permanently in the early 2000s.

"It was harder than you'd ever imagine being on the road," she says of the WWE schedule. "We'd be on the road for two months straight, with a three-day break to do our laundry back home in between trips. Back then, you looked for laundromats on the road. But now they're

---

[4]Note: This sounded totally creepy to me, but she seemed excited about it.
[5]This was the WWE's version of the Oscars, but the concept, which included lame skits and an awards presentation, lasted only a few years.

on for three days, off for three days. It's much easier now. But Vince McMahon treated me like a daughter. He was the best boss I ever had, though most people can't stand him. I got paid well and got to see the world." It has been nearly a decade since she worked for the WWE, but recently made a guest appearance on *Monday Night Raw* and appears to be trying to set the table for a return. "You never know," she says. "Who knows what the future holds? I hear rumors, and the rumors are good."

Sytch had no sports background, besides cheerleading ("I was captain of the team in high school and college"), prior to beginning her wrestling experiences 18 years ago. She has no plans to do anything else. "After doing something for 18 years, it's all you know," she says, though I can imagine that the wrestling world isn't kind to women who aren't young, new, and beautiful. "It just seems like the thing to do." She was, however, an excellent student. "I was a pre-med major at the University of Tennessee, and was undecided between orthopedics and plastic surgery," she says. "When I was working for Smoky Mountain on the weekends, I got discovered by Vince McMahon and dropped out of school. I was working part time, trying to make a buck or two here or there. The rest is history."

She says this, the history part, with a tinge of fatigue and regret. She got the call from McMahon a month before she was to graduate with her bachelor's degree. I ask her about this. "No, no regrets ... but sure, wouldn't everybody want to be called Dr. So and So? I'd love to be Dr. Sytch right now."

CHAPTER 7

Nikita Koloff Is Minnesota's Best Angry Russian

"For I know the plans I have for you," declares the LORD, "plans to prosper you and not to harm you, plans to give you hope and a future."

—Jeremiah 29:11

Nikita Koloff made his living in the deception business, and is now, ironically, making his living trying to get people to understand the gospel of Jesus Christ. Koloff, 49, came from that selfsame Robbinsdale, Minnesota, cradle[1] of ethnic heels that produced evil German Baron Von Raschke, and he held the NWA's National Heavyweight, U.S. Heavyweight, and World Heavyweight belts before hanging up the tights at the relatively young age of 33.

Koloff wrestled in a black singlet and, unlike some of his other evil Russian counterparts, actually looked somewhat evil, if not Russian. He sported a shaved head and goatee, years before every tough guy everywhere sported a shaved head and goatee and, in fact, may have had a hand in ushering in that look. Koloff's real name is, now, Koloff, as he had it legally changed some years ago from his given name

---

[1]Robbinsdale, Minnesota, also produced "Mr. Perfect" Curt Hennig, "Ravishing" Rick Rude, Tom Zenk, and Krusher Kruschev.

Nelson Scott Simpson. Simpson was a standout football player who was on his way toward a USFL tryout in 1984 when wrestling intervened, and he was introduced to the business by fellow Minnesotan Road Warrior Animal.

"Animal played on the same college football team I did," he says. The two played at Golden Valley Lutheran Community College, which, Koloff is quick to point out, was known at the time for being the number-one junior college football program in the nation. "He (Animal) called and said the promoter asked him if he had any buddies from the football team who could shave their heads and be an evil Russian. He immediately gave them my name, and the next day I was packing my car and driving to a strange town to meet the promoter. I had no wrestling experience, amateur or professional, and that day I met the world tag team champions and spent three hours on an interview set."

The storyline, hatched by Don Kernodle and Sgt. Slaughter, called for Koloff to play a Russian who was supposed to participate in the upcoming Olympics, but was scared off by the potential Russian boycott. He would then join forces with his "uncle" Ivan Koloff, another big, scary Russian who would turn out to be considerably less big and scary than Koloff.

The beauty of playing a big, scary Russian is that often, you don't have to do anything except stand there and look mean, which is exactly what Koloff did, initially. His matches were short, his debut requiring all of 11 seconds, and his early interviews required nothing more than standing in the background and looking mean. This is a good place to comment on how articulate Koloff is and how kind-sounding his voice is. This is in stark contrast to the gravelly rasp that most wrestlers feel the need to effect in most of their for-wrestling interactions. Koloff's voice is an odd combination of two dialects—Mid-Atlantic South and upper Midwest.

"I wrestled the night after I got into town, and they showed me one or two things and threw me in on a sold-out television taping card," he recalls. "The promoter said that if I tripped over the ropes, I was fired, but I was fairly confident that I could get through it without tripping over the ropes."

Koloff survived two "Joe Theisman fractures"[2] on both legs during his college football career, which started at Golden Valley Lutheran and ended at Morehead State in Kentucky. Though he was being tracked by NFL scouts and grooming for the ill-fated USFL, Koloff dropped football immediately to pursue the wrestling opportunity full force.

"I stopped watching football completely," he says, when asked if he regretted trading the competition of football for wrestling's staged storylines. "But wrestling was still very competitive, especially in what I'll call the old-school era. If you didn't perform, you were very replaceable in that era. You could go from being a main event guy to a mid-card guy, to a prelim guy in a very short amount of time. Every night, my goal was to have people walking out of the arena feeling like they'd gotten their money's worth."

In the early days, Koloff and his colleagues were paid based on how many butts they put in the seats. Sometimes his paycheck for an evening of work would barely reach $50. We discuss, briefly, the amounts of money being made by current wrestlers, many of whom are in their forties, age-wise, and if Koloff ever regrets the seemingly huge amounts of money left in the ring for the parade of shaven-headed Koloff derivatives[3] to snatch up. "I was in a prison recently in Nassau, Bahamas," he says, shifting gears. "I had the opportunity to share the gospel with all of the inmates there, and saw 50 men and women literally take a stand for the gospel and put their faith in Christ, in a place where they'll no doubt face great persecution. You can't put a price tag on that experience . . . I mean, how much is a soul worth?"

****

We talk briefly about many of the common pitfalls associated with a life in wrestling, of which Koloff figures he's "probably watched a total of 20 hours" in the last 15 years. "A number of the guys from my era have died for multiple reasons—drug overdoses, heart failure, suicide," he says. "It's a lot of pressure, traveling all day and wrestling

---

[2]These are, simply, compound fractures—the one where the bone ends up poking through the skin—of the lower leg, named after Washington Redskins quarterback Joe Theisman's especially disgusting fracture at the hands of Lawrence Taylor (who, it should be added, has done a little bit of professional wrestling himself).

[3]Namely, Bill Goldberg, who looked so much like Nikita Koloff at the beginning of his heralded wrestling career, that I actually thought he *was* Nikita Koloff.

all night. And whatever they choose to relieve their pressures with usually turns out to be a bad choice.

"And there's this façade of friendship and camaraderie within wrestling that is, for the most part, false," he says. "There are guys who are willing to do and say anything to get into that top spot. You develop rapport with one or two guys, but friendship is a fallacy, not reality.

"But the biggest pitfall in my opinion is that many guys buy into their own advertising. That is, they start believing they *are* the characters they're portraying."

And what they're portraying, for the most part, are chest-poundingly buffoonish characters who, by nature of what makes them popular to wrestling fans, are going to be poorly equipped to deal with the challenges of real life. But the line between fakery and reality in wrestling is just blurred enough that the wrestlers can cave to the temptation to take their characters outside the ring. In fact, in most cases, that is encouraged by promoters. Koloff himself was fairly famous for staying "in character" outside the ring, and the stories of characters like "The Million Dollar Man" Ted DiBiase throwing money around in real life to enhance his character. It is those characters who, generally, have allowed wrestlers like Koloff and DiBiase to continue generating income post-career.

"I've been fortunate to have had a hand, by the grace of God, in a number of wrestlers coming to know the Lord," he says. "A lot of them have read my books or heard me preach. But other guys, like Ric Flair, run as fast as they can the other way." It's Flair who provided, according to Koloff, some of his greatest memories in wrestling. "Ric was masterful," he says, "the consummate wrestler." The two squared off in the first-ever Great American Bash in 1985. "I was still a greenhorn only 13 months into the business, but I'd already held the world six-man tag title, and now I was wrestling Flair for the world heavyweight title."

Watching those old matches, I'm struck by the images of a prime Ric Flair, who has been around so long that it's difficult to remember what he looked like in eras gone by. Koloff, by contrast, was huge and thickly muscled—possessing the same outsized traps and pecs that would later make wrestlers like Goldberg and Batista famous. And there's a certain genius to his fast-twitch, jerky movements in the ring. His movements look somehow less "American" than those of his opponent. Their match is marked by a slowness of tempo common to matches in that era, but when Koloff struck, he did so in relatively explosive fashion.

Koloff also had a memorable best-of-seven series against a spectacularly mulleted babyface named Magnum T. A., who was as big and popular as any babyface in wrestling before a severe car accident prematurely ended his career. Their series took place during the Great American Bash Tour of 1986, and would culminate with a Russian, Koloff, winning the U.S. Heavyweight Title in their rubber match.

T. A. had bleached-blonde hair and a moustache reminiscent of that of his namesake, Magnum P.I., and both men were huge and ripped. So huge and ripped, in fact, that they were two of a handful of NWA wrestlers who could have easily been headliners in the WWF[4], which, at the time, was in the midst of proving its superiority with events like Wrestlemania. By today's standards, their matches were slow, often utilizing a series of lockups and chain maneuvers for the first five minutes of action. Two other things stand out about their matches—one involves one of my few enduring memories of the NWA, and that is a forehead full of blood matting down blonde hair. The NWA loved blonde babyfaces almost as much as it loved bloody matches. The other is the fact that the NWA didn't utilize mats around the ring, so that when wrestlers were tossed out, as Magnum T. A. was often during the series, they landed on hard arena-floor concrete.

As the mid-eighties gave way to the late eighties, and the era of evil Russians was drawing to a close amidst the growing popularity of Mikhael Gorbachev, the NWA's Dusty Rhodes saw an opportunity to turn the popular Koloff "babyface," and the American Dream and the Russian Nightmare united for a series of memorable tag matches.

Koloff retired at the relatively young age of 33 and, except for a few cameos and some independent stuff, didn't return to the ring. "I'm sort of known as the Barry Sanders of wrestling," he says, of retiring in one's prime like the legendary NFL running back. "As a youngster, my passion was football, and I always said I would walk away on top, with people wanting more. I always had an aversion to the guys that hung around a year or two too long. But as far as what I do now, my wrestling notoriety has given me a far bigger platform than I would have had, even if I had played for a few years in the NFL. To my

---

[4]Koloff was reportedly offered a deal with McMahon and the WWF shortly after his first Bash appearance with Flair, but declined in favor of the T. A. storyline.

knowledge, nobody ever came in the way I did, or walked away in the prime of their career."

****

Koloff is primarily a father and a speaker now, and says that life on the road in wrestling, which was a constant repetitive cycle of flying on planes, renting cars, and staying in hotels, has prepared him very well for his life as a roving evangelist, in which he regularly does the same things. His children, who were for the most part too young to be very engaged in the reality of their father's career, know his alter ego only through videotapes and the reactions of fans. "To them, I'm just dad," he says. For the record, he has never been to Russia, his billed country of origin, but was in Moldova briefly on a missions trip, where he said that for the most part he went unrecognized.

"I was trying to figure out what life held for me," Koloff says of the time immediately following his retirement from the ring.

> I owned a gym, and I had this fame from my quote, unquote[5] 'career' in wrestling, but I knew that there had to be more to life than this. I was invited to a church in Concord, North Carolina, and accepted the invitation. The question was asked at the end of the service, 'Has anyone here not given their life to Christ?' I had a head knowledge of Jesus Christ and of the basics of Christianity, but I guess you could say on that day I made it personal.
>
> But the most interesting part is what happened after the service. I was approached by an elderly man who was obviously in failing health. He said that he wasn't a wrestling fan at all, but had seen me on television, on a wrestling program, five years previous. He said that he felt the Holy Spirit moving him to pray for my salvation that day, and he continued doing so, faithfully, for the next five years. Even though he was sick, he said he felt compelled to come to church that morning. He sat in back, but said that he immediately knew who I was as soon as I came forward. And I thought that of all the churches in the world, how amazing it was that the Lord sent me to his church, and to the service he attended.

Koloff went on to explain that the Lord has given him a passion for world missions, and his goal is to continue to visit nations he's never

---

[5] I find it interesting that Koloff says "quote, unquote" when referring to his career in wrestling, which suggests that even wrestlers—at least the mentally healthy ones—refer to their own careers and accomplishments with a sense of self-satire or irony.

visited, and to eventually plant a church. None of this, he says, would have been possible without the platform that his strange career afforded him. "The wrestling gig was God's sense of humor," he explains. "Honestly, the idea of two sweaty guys grabbing ahold of each other was not real appealing to me."

CHAPTER 8

Leveling Up: Training, Continued

I have the flu tonight (fever, chills) but am driving to Coldwater anyway, partly because I don't want to shirk my responsibility to drive Lewis, and partly because I don't want to run the risk of falling woefully behind my classmates. I am already dreading the bumping, and tell Lewis that my 31-year-old body is finally starting to rebel against all of the abuse and punishment it's taken over the years.

The weather always sucks on this drive. Tonight it is 44 degrees with a driving rain, making the already unappealing hour drive that much more aggravating.

"Did you hear that Bri 2 Fly quit?" Lewis asks. He's disappointed because Bri 2 Fly was his main training partner and often worked with him in the EWF shows. Apparently, Bri 2 Fly has decided to move to Florida to work, with his girlfriend, as a fitness trainer on a cruise ship, which sounds infinitely more appealing than paying a large monthly fee to drive through hellish Michigan weather to take bumps every Monday and Wednesday night. I don't give voice to the fact that I think Bri got the better end of this deal, because I can tell that Lewis is disappointed.

I feel tingly and achy during the warm-up portion of our workout, and figure that I will get through this part, go to the bathroom to throw up, and then put on my hoodie, slump on a bench, and wait for the two hours to click away before collecting Lewis to go home. My dilemma with Price of Glory is that because they are so exacting in their standards, it will probably be several months before I actually get in the ring in a real match, which means I need to keep the lines of communication open with Pro Championship Wrestling in Chicago. This makes every practice important.

After warm-ups, we learn the body slam, which feels like something of a graduation for me out of chain wrestling and into actual bigger spots. Much like it sounds, the slam involves lifting another wrestler over your shoulder and then driving him down, back-first, onto the mat. Adrenaline kicks in, and for the time being my body forgets that it has the flu and focuses on the task of lifting Tim, a 230-pound forklift operator from Battle Creek, over my shoulder.

The idea with the body slam is for the slamee to hop a little bit, called a feed, into the maneuver, posting his right hand on the left hip of the guy doing the slamming to help diminish some of the body weight. Surprisingly, I am soon hefting Tim up onto my shoulder and slamming him onto the mat with relative ease. The important part of the landing is that the guy being slammed hits the mat with the broad part of his back—landing on either shoulder, or even on the lower part of the back will cause real pain and probably real injury.

After body slams, it is onto the hip toss, and time for me to confront my fear of doing flips. I realized shortly into this endeavor that wrestling is pretty much all about doing flips and, further, that my body has never actually done this—not even into a swimming pool. The hip toss basically involves the tossee running and doing a front bump (front flip) onto the mat. The visual here is that he hooks arms with the guy doing the tossing, and the result is a nice, big-looking move.

Again, I'm paired with Tim, a really nice guy whose 230 pounds is beginning to wreak havoc on my already football-gimpy right shoulder. After tossing him a few times, I take my running flips onto the crash pad, which is essentially a bigger, softer mat that provides a much safer place to land than the wrestling mats along the floor. It takes about one flip to make me really thankful for the crash pads, and really anxious about doing this on the floor mats next week. It's a strange feeling, going head over heels, but one I'm glad to have mastered, at least in part.

****

I haven't trained in two weeks. I've battled the Michigan winter flu, and the Michigan winter in general—as most of last week the road to

Coldwater was impassable. Truth be told, it's kind of been a relief not to go to wrestling. While I enjoy the training, I'm not sure I have it in me to really embrace this. Lewis, who works two day jobs at Abercrombie & Fitch and Dick's Sporting Goods, tells me that during his shifts, he often does nothing but think about new "spots." "At Abercrombie I'm really just standing there for four hours and occasionally folding shirts," he explains. "All I do at home is watch wrestling videos, so when I go into work I'm constantly thinking about new spots, and new chain[1] stuff to try."

Lewis will spend most of tonight's training session "chaining" with Jack—the blonde student from Grand Valley State University, who I learn is double-majoring in Spanish and Arabic, and whose parents don't know he's training to become a pro wrestler. "It hasn't come up," he says. This kind of secretiveness is a common theme among the trainees. Being into wrestling is not unlike being into role-playing games—it's not something you generally talk about with the public. Wrestlers tend to be focused only on wrestling. There is no talk of the Super Bowl, the Pistons, presidential primaries, or any other aspect of sports, politics, or life for that matter. It is only tapes, YouTube clips, spots, and storylines.

We'll be trained tonight by a guy named Money Mike, who has wrestled for Price of Glory in the past, and is also training to be a MMA fighter. Money Mike, a 23-year-old black guy from Georgia, moved up here solely to train at Severn's school and works the graveyard shift doing maintenance at a movie theater in Coldwater. His record is 16–1 as an amateur fighter, and he holds a couple of titles in the 155-pound weight class.

Money Mike's home is a bunk bed in the back of the facility. "I'm looking forward to getting my own place," he says. Mike has lived here for two years, and has his first professional MMA fight in April. Tonight he's teaching us suplexes and chain stuff. His practices are much more laid back than Abercrombie's, to say the least. He pulls out the crash pads (thank you, Money Mike) and we begin to work on suplexes and throws.

---

[1]Chain wrestling is generally considered old-school and takes place more on the independent circuit than in the WWE at this point. You hardly ever see it in WWE shows because, in general, fans don't want to see it.

The suplex requires that both men work in unison, as the guy taking the suplex basically jumps and does a front (flip) bump while the other guy appears to lift him by the trunks. It's a fun move, and doesn't hurt at all when performed on the crash pads.

Money Mike's ring persona is that of a brash, hip-hop character who flashes gold teeth and bling-bling around the ring. His real-life persona couldn't be further from this. He is almost timid when talking to the class, and only seems comfortable when he is giving or taking moves. That's when he comes alive. Mike's 150 pounds soars through the air with relative ease, and I am thankful to not be hefting Tim's 230 pounds around tonight.

"Would you like to try a suplex," asks Money Mike. He says this so softly that I think he's almost whispering.

****

I've decided what it is about wrestling: It's not fun, which is completely counterintuitive. You would think taking on a different persona, putting on tights, and jumping around a ring goofing off would be a blast. But it usually isn't. Many wrestlers, and wrestling people, view the whole thing with a really grim sense of determination and resolve. There's very little whimsey. No playfulness.[2] They take this stuff really, really seriously. I both do get it[3] and don't get it, if that makes any sense.

Mark Pennington scolded me again for not coming to the Price of Glory show on Sunday. Truth be told, after taking in a couple of other indie shows, I can't bring myself to do it again. It was too depressing. There's always a good reason not to make the hour-plus drive down to Coldwater. Going to certain indie wrestling shows, for me, is kind of like making yourself volunteer at a nursing home—you know you're not going to like what you see there, and you know that, more often than not, you'll go home feeling sad. "It's part of paying your dues," explains Pennington, of attending the POG shows. This, apparently, is in addition to the actual financial dues that I pay each month. He's right, but I still can't bring myself to go.

I find out from Jack that Tim, the big forklift driver from Battle Creek, quit last week. Tim and Bri 2 Fly are gone, and I haven't seen

---

[2]The most successful promoters, like Rick Jenig, get the joke, but still respect their audiences.

[3]I get it in the sense that if it's not taken seriously, people could get hurt.

James, the trainee from Detroit, in a while, either. It's an attrition thing. It's hard to make the drive. It's hard to go home with the bumps and bruises.

Wrestling is hard on the head, itself. Nearly every move involves either snapping the head over, or the head hitting the mat. It's a very different "hard" from football, where your head is hitting other people, but it's also in a helmet. I realize I have a low-grade headache almost every night after wrestling practice. Tonight is no different, with snap mares[4] and headlock takeovers[5] on the agenda. I'm working with Jack, and we each do what seems like about a hundred reps apiece on these two moves, before "bumping out"[6] at the end of practice.

There's a new guy in the car tonight, named Mosi. He's a big black guy with dreads who will be joining us in class tonight. Mosi, I learn, has been in the business for several years, and though he is from Detroit, he has moved around quite a bit, wrestling in southern California before moving back to the area. He's also the first wrestler I've interviewed for this project who is comfortable talking about something besides wrestling—we have long discussions on books, films, and other sports. He also recently wrestled his first hard-core match.

"When you go to shows, always have your gear[7] in your car," he explains, "because you never know when you'll get the chance to work." He goes on to tell the story of a show he worked in the Detroit area, where he found out he would not only be on the card, but he would be working a "Death Match." His ring handle, appropriately, is Mo Dread. "I'd never worked a hard-core match before so I was a little freaked out, but I think I kept my poker face on pretty well."

Driving, I ask Mosi what kinds of accessories there were in the ring. I can't believe I'm having this conversation. "There was a baseball bat

---

[4]One guy stands in front of another guy and pretends to whip him over by the head. The guy getting snap-mared basically just does a front flip bump down to the mat.

[5]Just like it sounds. The guy taking the move is in a side headlock, and the guy giving the move basically drops to his knees and whips the other guy over his back. For some reason, this hurts more than the snap-mares.

[6]Ten reps each of front bumps, side bumps, face bumps, and back bumps.

[7]Mosi tells the story of living in a seedy part of San Diego, near strip clubs and adult novelty stores. "There were the best places to get wrestling gear made," he explains, ostensibly because there is already a large supply of brightly colored spandex available to make costumes for the strippers. This makes me almost unbearably sad. I imagine him taking his hard-earned money down to the booty-shaking district in search of the perfect pair of electric blue tights.

wrapped in barbed wire, some thumbtacks[8] on the mat, some halogen
tubes, a ladder, and a mirror," he explains, in a tone of voice sug-
gesting that I just asked him what he had for dinner or something
equally humdrum. I try to get my mind around the fact that somewhere, at some point, a wrestling promoter thought "this would be
much more entertaining if there were thumbtacks and shards of glass
all over the ring." Why not, I wonder to myself, just hang a gun from
a rope in the rafters? Whichever wrestler reaches it first can use it to
shoot and kill the other wrestler, thereby winning the match.

"It wasn't that bad, but it was the first time I got a scar from a wrestling match. I was supposed to take a bump and get pinned on a ladder,
but before that happened, I saw the guy drag the mirror over on top of
it. I just took a deep breath and took the bump on the mirror, which was
on top of the ladder. After the pinfall, I just laid there for a minute and
wiggled around to make sure there was no glass stuck in my body. I
had a pretty deep gash on my arm, but it was more like a bad scrape
than a gash. When I got home, I figured my wife[9] would be mad so I
just tacked the 50 dollars up on the bulletin board, so that it would be
the first thing she saw when she walked in."

****

ON WRESTLING, PYRO, AND DECEPTION: A WRESTLEMANIA XXIV INTERLUDE

By now it's no secret that wrestling, essentially, is based on a fundamental lie. Granted, it's a fundamental lie that most of us, by fourth
grade or so, knew was a lie but willingly accepted because it was fun
to do so in the presence of other people. We knew, intuitively, that
Hulk Hogan couldn't slam Andre the Giant without a good bit of help
from the Giant, who weighed upwards of 540 pounds at his heaviest.
We also knew, when we saw close-ups of Hogan trapping a man in
the corner, hopping on a turnbuckle, and "punching" him, that he
wasn't actually punching him. We could see with our own eyes that
the punches weren't connecting.

---

[8]Why thumbtacks? "Sunday! Sunday ... Sunday! At the Backwater Civic War Memorial
Veterans Elks Lodge Auditorium ... it's a Random Office Supplies DEATH MATCH!
Featuring fax machines, filing cabinets, staplers and manila file folders!"

[9]He has been married for several years, and has a three-year-old daughter. He's also a stay-
at-home dad.

Still, you get the right mix of people in the room—people willing to suspend disbelief for a couple of hours—and this became very exciting. It's this dynamic—untruth—that has made it so difficult to get interviews for this project, because at whatever point the audience (if, in this case, the audience is a writer) suspends belief, the wrestler not only loses control, but loses the ability to make the activity (he feels) fun or interesting for anyone. That's why when you see wrestlers out among the general public, it is often a disappointing or less-than-exciting experience. Strip them of their makeup, spandex, and television cameras, and they become very ordinary.

I've had two such experiences, one of which[10] happened recently at a Burger King in Lansing, Michigan. There, I ended up in line behind Sabu. As a wrestler, Sabu was billed from Bombay, India, or at times Saudi Arabia, which made it seem all the stranger to see him at a Burger King in Lansing. In real life, his name is Terry Brunk, and he was born in Staten Island, New York, if Wikipedia is to be believed.

Anyway, it took it a few minutes to register that I was in line behind Sabu. At first I thought he was just a shortish (Sabu is probably 5′10″ or so), middle-aged guy with shaved forearms (true), a tan, and a pretty ripped physique. In other words, I figured he was a local bodybuilder because he and the guy he was with—another huge guy I didn't recognize—were trying to decide what to order off the ultra-fatty Burger King menu and discussing things like protein content and grams of carbohydrates. Then I saw the bladed forehead, full of scar tissue, under a WWE ballcap and recognized his prominent nose. I also realized he walked with the gait of someone who had spent the majority of his younger years crashing through tables and falling from high places

---

[10]The other happened when I was a child in Hartford City, Indiana (population: about 7,000). I was in grade school, and my dad and I went to one of the only car dealerships in town to look at cars. We were greeted by a huge, muscular guy with reddish hair and a beard. As it turns out, this guy was one of the "Moon Dogs"—a tag team that enjoyed a small window of popularity during the early 1980s, winning a WWF/E tag title in 1981. He was Moondog Rex (real name Randy Colley), and his tag partner—Moondog Spot—would later garner fame by dying of a heart attack in the ring during one of Jerry Lawler's wrestling shows. Anyway, Moondog Rex had that big, florid, post-steroidal look that a lot of not-quite-young former strength athletes tend to have, and I thought he was really cool, not yet aware that selling cars in my tiny Indiana hometown might not have a whole lot of future in it. We went back a few days later to look at the car again, and Moondog Rex had moved on—apparently to continue his wrestling career, which lasted until the early 1990s.

onto his back. He walked like a man who was in his seventies—sort of shuffly and wobbly like your grandpa after 50 years on the assembly line. This makes sense, in part, because Sabu is known not only for hard core (explained before), but for a unique, high-flying style that often involves jumping off chairs and then the ropes before finally landing on the other person. He is also known for, among other things, taping a broken jaw shut to finish a match, and also taping a ripped bicep together, again, so that he could finish a match and not miss any time due to the injury.

Sabu is also known for getting his neck broken a lot, which, in the pantheon of things to be known for, would be pretty low on my list. However, even the neck breaks are semilegendary. I watch video of one in which Sabu is dragon-plexed through a standard folding table which was sitting kitty-corner, semi-upright in one of the ring corners. While I won't—can't—really explain the physics behind the dragon-plex in great detail, suffice it to say that it looks like the type of thing that you almost can't do without breaking your neck. His other broken neck came in an ECW match against Chris Benoit, back in what looked to be an especially ripped time for Benoit, all steroid allegations aside. Just a minute or so into their match, Benoit hit what looked to be a really awkward back drop that had Sabu crashing to the mat, basically right on his head. Sabu immediately rolled out of the ring and was attended to by somebody at ringside. The dilemma created, of course, by these wrestling broken necks is that the crowd, wrestlers, and referee all come to the realization that it's a real injury at different times, or sometimes never. They are so used to seeing wrestlers roll out of the ring with various contrived injuries, that when a real one happens, it's almost startling to see everybody accept it differently. Benoit started playing to the crowd, but then seemed to stop and just sort of stand there after realizing the seriousness of the injury.[11]

Sabu is also pretty famous in wrestling circles for a barbed-wire matchup with wrestling legend Terry Funk,[12] wherein the wrestling ring ropes were replaced with barbed wire. If this sounds disgusting, and if you haven't seen it, it is in fact disgusting. Sabu and Funk hit a variety of moves in the middle of the ring for a few minutes before

---

[11]I could be wrong about this. It could have been a fake broken neck, but it looked pretty real to my untrained eye.

[12]Sabu's real name is Terry Brunk, which sounds a lot like Terry Funk.

Sabu is launched headlong into the barbed wire. He's then Irish-whipped into the barbed wire ropes on one occasion, and then atomic-dropped over the ropes on another occasion. After this atomic drop, his crotch literally has to be untangled from the top rope/wire. The crowd is chanting "Sabu" at this most pivotal crotch-untangling moment, and they (crowd) have a real "ancient Rome" feel about them, like these would be the same people, centuries ago, who would have cheered for a lion to eat a person for their entertainment. Funk is then whipped into the barbed wire, which Sabu uses to tie him up. I try, for a moment, to envision the production meeting in which all parties involved thought this was a good idea. The announcer on the broadcast utters perhaps the most obvious statement ever uttered, when he explains, "this is a bloodbath." Yeah. It's later in this match that Sabu famously had his bicep ripped open and then subsequently taped back together in what was a great piece of live television. Most impressively, he keeps taping the bicep together while at the same time receiving a neck-breaker onto a chair. The announcer declared, "This is just getting difficult to watch," and "This match will leave Sabu scarred both mentally and physically." I'm still having a hard time with the conversation that probably went something like: "Yeah, so after I wrap you in barbed wire and lay you out on a table at ringside, I'll then wrap my own midsection in barbed wire, and then jump on you, on the table, which will then break and send us both careening to the floor."[13]

Anyway, Sabu's signature long, black hair was tied back in a ponytail that hung out the back of the ball cap, and he wore a white, linen Japanese-ish sort of dress shirt with black dress pants and black loafers. It was a dressed-up look, except for the ball cap. Like wrestling itself, it seemed well thought out but still, somehow, tacky. Somewhat lost in all of this, however, is the fact that Sabu was/is one of the most talented, athletic wrestlers in the history of the sport. His jumps from chair to rope to ring floor were among the most, well, beautiful and graceful maneuvers in wrestling. He routinely did things in the ring that most people couldn't or wouldn't do, which makes him an important and respected part of the sport's history.

---

[13]This whole thing took place at a venue called the ECW Arena, which was actually a place that was really an old warehouse called Viking Hall on the south side of Philadelphia. If wrestling has taught us anything, it's that anytime you put chairs and a ring anyplace, that place can then be called an "arena."

My wife asked me why I didn't interview Sabu. To be honest, it was a mixture of fear, plus the realization that it is often more fun just to watch people like that from afar. Fear, because he looked sort of upset and agitated, and rather than make him mumble through an interview, I could just watch him out of his natural environment. Fear, also, because this guy has done some of the most insane stuff in the history of mankind, not to mention professional wrestling. There aren't a whole lot of people around who think it's a good idea to swaddle themselves in barbed wire and then wrestle. This particular Burger King had a television up high in a corner, which was playing a Hillary Clinton campaign speech; for what it's worth, Sabu seemed completely uninterested, though much of the rest of the restaurant watched her intently. I wondered, at this point, if he was upset that nobody was recognizing him.

This gave me a chance to explain my "Fame and Interviews" theory to my wife, which basically explains that if the celebrity is truly washed up, then they are more than happy—probably thrilled—to be recognized in public and asked for an interview. However, if they are almost washed up or in the B-list category, they can often be very difficult or downright prickish in public situations. I'm guessing this may be Sabu's stage of life, though I'm not completely sure.

****

The night after the Sabu sighting, I am back at my buddy Vandermolen's apartment for Wrestlemania XXIV.[14] I enter to find Nick and 10 buddies all shirtless[15] on an assortment of sofas. His ever-present pile of laundry is still there in the corner, and a large television is the focal point. There are even sheets of paper on the walls listing each match, and each person's prediction for that match. They go big for Wrestlemania. Though the event just started, a large pile of empty pizza boxes is in the kitchen.

One of the tenets of Wrestlemania is "pyro,"[16] as in the fireworks that accompany each wrestler when they enter the ring, the fireworks that signal the beginning of the show, and the fireworks that happen

---

[14]Though the WWE has a pay-per-view event nearly every month, Wrestlemania is by far the biggest, and is a Super Bowl of sorts for the organization. Hence the roman numerals.
[15]My friend J. R.'s girlfriend described it as "lots of skinny, white-boy flesh."
[16]According to the *Orlando Sentinel,* the WWE spent nearly $300,000 on the pyro for Wrestlemania XXIV.

at random intervals throughout the show. We would wake the next morning to find that a broken cable resulted in 40 or so wrestling fans being burned by falling purple and gold embers, as some of the fireworks misfired into the crowd.

Wrestlemania has changed a great deal since its inception in 1985. The first Wrestlemania happened at the height of wrestling's mainstreamness, and seemed to capture the attention of real celebrities— with Liberace, Muhammad Ali, Billy Martin, Cyndi Lauper, and the Rockettes all playing a role, as well as then-TV star Mr. T, who tagged with Hulk Hogan against Rowdy Roddy Piper and Paul Orndorff. Hogan was at the height of his mainstream stardom at this time, having just appeared in *Rocky III* as a character named Thunderlips, who was basically just a caricature of Hogan, who is himself a caricature of someone from California who is really tan, strong and confident. As a child, I wasn't so much a fan of Hogan as I was fascinated by his celebrity. By simply widening his eyes, shaking, and ripping off his yellow shirt, he made disciples of the masses. Apparently, even though we were at the height of our military and economic power as a nation, we still needed a hero. In the fashion of most true, American celebrities, we now get to watch him deteriorate before our eyes—a shrinking old man in red tights and bleach-blonde hair. But in a way, this is right. Where else would old television creations live out their years, besides on television?

Back then, most of the matches were normal, meaning the WWF hadn't yet discovered the magic of tables, ladders, and chairs as a staple of pay-per-view matches, nor had they begun putting "announcer's tables" at ringside for the sole purpose of being smashed into, destroyed, and then used as weapons.

By contrast, this year's Wrestlemania started with a "Belfast Brawl," featuring an Irish character named Finlay squaring off against sometime wrestler/sometime announcer John Bradshaw Layfield (JBL). The match featured the wrestlers hitting each other with, among other things, a cookie sheet, a garbage can, and a ladder. It also featured a little person (Hornswoggle) who also got hit several times with the aforementioned garbage can. Now, far be it from me to argue for "purity" in my make-believe sports, but the gimmick matches get pretty old, pretty quickly. The next match was a ladder affair in which the winning wrestler (CM Punk) had to scale a ladder to pull a briefcase full of cash down from a dangling cable. As you can imagine, in the time it took for that to happen, most wrestlers were pounded by said ladders and/or hurled out of the ring from great heights through tables placed at ringside. There was also a monumental nut shot[17] that elicited howls of pain from those in the apartment. There was also a match featuring female wrestlers that had posed in *Playboy,* and a match featuring a boxer (Floyd Mayweather) against a wrestler (Big Show).

While there's nothing new about the champion-boxer-turned-pro-wrestler gimmick—for example, Muhammad Ali vs. Antonio Inoki—this iteration of it was every bit as cringe-worthy as Ali's attempt, but for different reasons. The main difference was that Mayweather fails to possess even a fraction of the charisma that Ali had, making his match with Big Show, and the stuff leading up to it, all the more painful to watch. What we all realized is that nobody likes Floyd Mayweather, and they probably never will. Or maybe it's just more appropriate to say that nobody cares about Floyd Mayweather, in a public sort of way. I'm sure family and friends care about him, but not the general public so much. By comparison, while half of America hated Ali with a red-hot passion, the other half loved him dearly. What was especially sad/funny about the Mayweather gimmick was his reliance on tired rap video style clichés to put his character over—large posse, brass knuckles, and a "Money May" persona that has included rap star 50 Cent in his posse. If the whole thing were kind of tongue-in-cheek self-satire, I would be much more comfortable with it, but I'm not sure it is. Mayweather, allegedly, made $20 million for the appearance.

The other interesting match of the evening (actually the de jure Main Event) features The Undertaker (Mark William Callaway), who at age 43 has been with WWF/E since I cared about wrestling the first time. Undertaker is more proof that the most popular figures in wrestling are mostly over the age of 40, which would be considered grotesquely over the hill in any other athletic endeavor. Still, for a big wrestler, Undertaker is surprisingly active and entertaining. He's also credited with originating several types of gimmick matches, including "Hell in a Cell" and the "Boiler Room Brawl." Undertaker began his career in 1984 in World Class Championship Wrestling in a match against Bruiser Brody. I was in the third grade and Randy Orton was four years old. Undertaker, like many older WWF/E stars, started as

---

[17]Wrestler falling from a 20-foot ladder, crotch first, onto one of the ring ropes.

a heel and made the switch to face, which leads me to believe that there's something going on within the wrestling fan's psyche that makes it hard to root against older people. Undertaker succeeds in part because his ring personas—specifically the tatted-up, biker, bad-ass thing—don't seem to deviate a whole lot from what's going on in his real life. Undertaker is a motorcycle and heavy-metal music enthusiast who once got the name of his second wife tattooed on his throat. That's commitment. The Undertaker is 6 feet 10 inches tall and weighs 295.

Tonight he'll face Edge (Adam Copeland) in a match that will put his 15-match Wrestlemania winning streak on the line. Reading a list of those victories, in fact, reads like a who's who of professional wrestling over a number of eras. In Wrestlemania VII, he dispatched Jimmy "Superfly" Snuka. In Wrestlemania VIII, it was Jake "The Snake" Roberts. In X8, he beat Ric Flair, and in Wrestlemania XX, it was Randy Orton. If true marquee staying power is the only real measuring stick of wrestling success, Undertaker has certainly achieved that.

Edge, his opponent, is himself not small (6′5″ and 250 pounds) and not young (35). But the blonde Edge's character has the ethos of youth, if not actual youth. His gear incorporates bright colors, as opposed to the differing shades of black appearing all over The Undertaker's body as both clothing and tattoos. If The Undertaker looks like the kind of huge, scary guy you'd meet in a biker bar, Edge looks like the kind of character one might meet at an 80s Night theme party. He once wrestled in tag teams known as "The Suicide Blondes" and "The Canadian Rockers."

Both of these wrestlers are good examples of a growing trend in wrestling, which is to create characters who don't have any qualities that are inherently face-like or heel-like, so that they can be flip-flopped between the two seemingly at will. Old babyfaces, like Bob Backlund and Hulk Hogan, played on the audience's level of trust for Americans, patriots, and clean-cut people. Heels, of course, used to do heelish things like bringing snakes into the ring,[18] chopping off people's hair,[19] or being foreign.[20] Now there are just two large, long-haired men in the ring who can do good or bad things, and seem to sometimes do both in large quantity.

---

[18]Jake "The Snake" Roberts.
[19]Brutus "The Barber" Beefcake.
[20]Nikolai Volkoff, Mr. Fuji.

Edge, though, seems good at being bad. First, it's easy to hate buff, blonde guys with long hair who seem arrogant. That part is simple. But Edge has also been a part of one of WWF/E's seedier and more soap-operaish storylines involving the real wife of the deceased Eddie Guerrero, Vickie, who is in a wheelchair and at different times either is or isn't going to marry Edge. Really, the only creative thing about the Edge character is his incorporation of the Edge Heads, or two other buff, blonde, long-haired guys who look exactly like him and run into the ring at opportune times to manipulate the outcomes of matches.

The upshot to the Edge/Undertaker matchup is that they're both big, active guys who can perform big moves and wrestle a long, entertaining match. This one is no disappointment. Early in the match the 6′ 10″ Undertaker flies over the top rope to jump on top of an outside-the-ring Edge. The match features a number of false finishes, including Edge surviving the Tombstone Piledriver to kick out after a referee sprints about a half a mile to get into the ring to replace the original, now-injured ref. After an intervention by the Edge Heads, Edge then hits a couple of spears[21] and then attempts to pin The Undertaker, thus breaking the streak. But the Undertaker instead throws on an awkward-looking Gogoplata[22] submission move causing Edge to tap out and thus lose his title. Cue more fireworks.

Other random funny things about Wrestlemania XXIV are:

> The "promo" that took place with WWE World Heavyweight[23] Champion Edge in which he describes "losing his innocence" as a child when he saw Hulk Hogan lose an early WM match. He then vowed that many of the children watching and in attendance that night would also lose their innocence which, oddly, proved to be true when several of them (children) were burned by WWE pyrotechnics.

> Ric Flair's robe. Flair would face Shawn Michaels in what would be his last match as a professional wrestler (until, probably, next month). He was resplendent in a blue robe, which didn't seem to have any entry or

---

[21]This move is just your good old, garden-variety football shoulder tackle.

[22]The Gogoplata actually comes from Brazilian jiu-jitsu and sometimes causes opponents to spit blood out of their mouths.

[23]If you're confused at this point, you're not alone. There is a World Heavyweight Championship, held by Edge, that he would lose later that night to the Undertaker. There is also a WWE Championship belt held by Randy Orton, that he would defend against John Cena and Triple H in a triple-threat match. There are so many titles that none of them mean anything. Of course, with this being pro wrestling, none of them mean anything, anyway.

exit point. We all wondered how he would get out of his robe to start the match, but in true attention-deficit fashion, all managed to miss him actually taking the robe off in the ring.

Ric Flair's age. Flair is 59 years old and was born in 1949, toward the beginning of Harry S. Truman's administration, before the Korean War, and before the popularization of television. He made his wrestling debut in 1972, when Richard Nixon was in office, which was also the year that DDT was banned as a pesticide. Oddly, the DDT[24] would become a popular wrestling finishing maneuver in the 1980s.

Ric Flair's skin. Flair's skin—shaven and tanned in true wrestling fashion —took on a purplish hue as the match with Michaels progressed, which caused a medical student in attendance to opine that Flair might actually be in the early stages of a heart attack.

The Flair/Michaels contest was clearly the de facto main event of the evening, which made it strange to see it buried in the middle of the card.[25] It's the only match that people were talking about beforehand, and probably the only one they'll really talk about afterward. The storyline is fairly simple—if Flair loses, then his seemingly endless career will finally be over. The WWE helped by running a montage of the contrived feud between Flair and Michaels, culminating in a bit where Michaels threatens to take Flair out behind the woodshed and then execute him like Old Yeller, which elicits a chuckle from around the room.

Ric Flair had a financial products company for a short time called Ric Flair Finance, whose tagline read that "we compete so that you don't have to." The company offered a "Figure Four Loan Process" that clients could use to get financing for cars, houses, and other material goods so that they could quote "live like Ric Flair." Ostensibly, the company's lifespan was short, as the link is now dead and only offers a contact page for Flair's agent, Elaine Gillespie, whose own Web site features a Flash animation of a robed Flair saying

---

[24]This is one of the least-cool popular moves in wrestling. All you do is put the opponent in a front facelock and then fall backward, so that the other guy basically takes a dive onto his forehead. It doesn't even look cool, but I guess the main upshot is that it's easy to perform. It's so lame that its uncoolness almost makes it cool (see also Ric Flair's knife-edge chop).
[25]The pacing of Wrestlemania XXIV's card was weird all the way around. The fact that this match took place before the Playboy Bunnies' match was downright bizarre. Ditto for the Floyd Mayweather/Big Show boxer-verus-giant-fat-guy sideshow match that has been done several times before.

"Woo" and other memorable catchphrases. Unfortunately, Flair's decision to enter the financial-products industry coincided with probably the worst economic crisis facing our nation since the Great Depression. Besides, it's probably difficult to enter a field that values being taken seriously after plying your trade in a profession that deals solely in deception. The Gillespie page touts Flair's 35 years in the ring and 16 world titles, and encourages bookings for "talk shows" and "motivational speaking."

Flair (Richard Morgan Fliehr) is probably the second-biggest celebrity, next to Hogan, to come out of professional wrestling, to date. However, it seems clear that he is having trouble turning that name and wrestling cache into mainstream dollars. Flair was born in 1949 in Edina, Minnesota, and eventually played offensive guard at the University of Minnesota, after a high school career as a two-time all-state lineman. Indeed to look at these late-sixties, early-seventies pictures of Flair is to look at a picture of someone who looks like a regular, Midwestern, beefy college jock. His face is rounder, and his muscles are bigger, than they were for most of his career. But like all great Minnesota wrestling legends, Flair realized that college jocks aren't very interesting, and tweaked his character accordingly.

Flair was the son of an obstetrician and a marketing executive; I'm certain the latter had a lot to do with Flair making and keeping himself marketable all those years without the built-in helps of freakish size/strength or otherwise freakish physical features. The fact is that I've seen Flair's signature strut imitated by men everywhere—from hardened immigrant construction workers to pasty-faced office workers. People either liked hating Ric Flair or they liked Ric Flair, but, more importantly to the marketer, they always paid money to see or listen to Ric Flair.

Flair had a brief AWA turn in the early 1970s before veering south to the Mid-Atlantic region where he was involved in a private plane crash that claimed the life of the pilot and left other wrestlers maimed or paralyzed. Flair himself broke his neck in three places and was reportedly told he would never wrestle again before reportedly returning to the ring in four (or six) months (depending on the source) after some rigorous physical therapy.

This is a good place to interject my amazement at the fact that many wrestlers continue in their careers after serious, potentially life-altering neck injuries. Seriously. You want to continue in a career that involves being pile-driven, hit upon the head with chairs and bodyslammed after already once breaking your neck? This is either extreme devotion or extreme stupidity. Maybe both. Either way, it's interesting.

This is also a good time to interject that, from an athletic standpoint, I respect the hell out of Ric Flair. Considering the fact that most NFL players have a four-year shelf life at best, the fact that Flair has stayed athletic and relevant for a seemingly endless string of decades is very significant. That, and I'm not sure how his body survived the whole thing, physically.

It's also a good time to interject that I'm currently trying to get an interview with Ric Flair, and negotiating that labyrinthine process that is The PR Agency gauntlet, including phone conversations and e-mails regarding a short interview with a person who, probably, isn't doing a whole lot else. I'd like to say that at this point in my career, I'm over being frustrated by this hoop-jumping, but that wouldn't be entirely true.

Flair won the NWA U.S. Heavyweight Championship from Bobo Brazil in 1977, but truly caught lightning in a bottle when he began referring to himself as The Nature Boy in 1978. In the early to mid-1980s, Flair was the NWA's franchise—an era that happened, for me, in a strange parallel universe of black-and-white magazine photos while I was watching the televised rise of the WWF/E. For me, the NWA was a product that happened in the South, and only there in black-and-white photos in rings that didn't look as sweet and arenas that didn't look as large as the WWF/E's. Still, Flair's accomplishments were very significant for kids in the South and for "real" wrestling fans everywhere.

His foil during this period was Dusty Rhodes, who was as fat and blue collar as Flair was blonde, tan, and successful-seeming. Rhodes used his everyman-ness to endear fans to him in a great example of how wrestling characters can be mutually beneficial. Flair's feud with Rhodes was as fundamental as any you see in real life: one good-looking a-hole with money and fame, and one sloppily endearing, funny, blue-collar guy with charisma who hates the good-looking a-hole.

Almost everybody likes Shawn Michaels. His "Sexy Boy" music is hilarious, but he is a top-notch technical guy and a great high-flyer despite his own age issues (at 43, he is a relative child compared to Flair). For that matter, everybody likes Flair too, mainly because he is a wrestling legend, and it's hard to root against a 59-year-old with a body that looks positively geriatric. Thus, this felt like one of those matches without a real bad guy.

I won't recount a blow-by-blow of the match here, except to say that it was great, and it included several figure-four leglocks (Flair's signature) and several instances of sweet chin music (Michaels's signature) as well as a moonsault (Michaels off the top rope, outside the ring onto a scorer's table). I think part of what I enjoyed the most about this match was its normalness—it started with a good bit of chaining, and then (besides Michaels crashing into an announcer's table) was devoid of any gimmicks. Flair was admirably spry for a man of his age, and Michaels was typically indestructible. He hit the table with such force that we were all convinced that he had broken some ribs.

It's at this point that I began to feel conflicted regarding the deceptive nature of wrestling. Because it is all a show, the emotion exhibited by Flair about his retirement could either be taken as sincere, and thus eliciting emotion in you, the viewer, or it could just be consumed cynically as another bit of wrestling showmanship, contrived for the fans. Ditto for Michaels's conflictedness over ending Flair's career with a series of Sweet Chin Musics.[26] Indeed, before Michaels landed the last of the musics to Flair's chin, he mouthed the words "I'm sorry" and "I love you" in Flair's direction and looked to be truly sincere when doing so. It's the kind of thing that would have made you really emotional were it real (imagine, now, Joe Frazier saying "I love you" to Muhammad Ali before blasting him with a left hook or Lawrence Taylor apologizing before concussing Joe Montana for the last time) and was still even a little bit emotional though the sport is fake. In fact, most of us in the room didn't know what to do with Flair's tears after the match, as well as the tears of his family collected at ringside. If we got emotional, we might feel like suckers for such a show of emotion. This, I think, is why adult wrestling fans are so, well, weird. The drama—both real and contrived—screws with your mind to such an extent that you don't know what is real[27] and what is just part of the show. You don't know when it's permissible to feel truly sad, so it's easier just to watch guys fly through tables.

---

[26]This is actually just a karate kick to the chin.

[27]Owen Hart's death, real, caused the same dilemma for wrestling fans, who, when coverage of that particular pay-per-view went dark, didn't know if they had truly witnessed something horrific, or if they had just witnessed another storyline twist, meant to build their anticipation for an upcoming match. Needless to say, this feeling isn't enjoyable, and it leaves fans feeling really screwed.

CHAPTER 9

The WWE Raw Wrestlemania Revenge House Show and the Strange Appeal of John Bradshaw Layfield

A guilty pleasure is something I pretend to like ironically, but in truth I just really like.

—Fargo Rock City

It's raining on an unseasonably cold spring day in East Lansing. I haven't been inside the Jack Breslin Student Events Center since going to watch the state high school basketball playoffs a few years previous, but it is a huge, clean, antiseptic college basketball venue (home to the Michigan State Spartans) that today hosts something called "Wrestlemania Revenge," put on by WWE Raw. It's strange to see such a clean, respectable venue hosting middle-aged men in T-shirts that read: "Randy Orton Rules, John Cena Drools," and the like. The fan population is diverse, though the common fashion thread seems to be to wear a lot of the color black. And whereas the "typical" Breslin Center crowd would consist of fresh-faced, affluent-looking youngsters, this crowd is discernibly rougher-looking, but in a way that is hard to describe. In fairness, though, I see a lot of families with young kids, and a young Asian family with a look that seems to scream "we're

PhD students." The man flexes his skinny arms for a photograph in front of the ring, smiling from ear to ear.

As for the ring itself, my friend J. R. comments on how much smaller it looks in real life. I think it's all a matter of context. You put the same ring in the middle of a poorly lit, dirty American Legion hall in a small town, and the scene looks scummy and depressing. Here, though, in the well-lit, gleamingly clean Breslin Center, it looks somehow majestic and full of possibilities.

There is a morbidly obese woman wearing a John Cena "54" jersey,[1] and a random, shirtless African American man wearing "Tapout" shorts and MMA gloves, with a championship belt of some kind slung over his shoulder. His look seems to say "I'm somebody, ask for my autograph," but nobody in our immediate vicinity seems to know who he is, and I will see him later, standing alone in the concourse with the belt still slung over his shoulder. I will feel a little sorry for him, but not sorry enough to go up and engage him in conversation. Says my friend Vandermolen: "I'm gonna become a celebrity so I can walk around shirtless," which is a little bit ironic, as Vandermolen routinely walks around shirtless in semipublic places anyway.

In the minutes before the opening bell at 5:00 p.m., Vandermolen, J. R., and I are deep in the throes of planning for the Literary Wrestling Alliance's one and only show. Being here for a live WWE event seems to have infused us with a new kind of creative energy. We have decided to do a magazine for the event, in the style of 80s pro wrestling magazines, with newsprint pages and poorly laid-out photographs. We're also planning a Web site with an intentionally bad 90s look about it, featuring teal on a black background. And mandatory mustaches for all heel characters.

We also remark on the omnipresent but still somehow unrecognizable rock music playing in the arena. It's all seemingly WWE-licensed music, and features heavy, clangy guitar riffs and screamy lyrics that all seem to revolve around two very masculine themes: Who the man is, and who your daddy is (also "sucking it").

The house lights go down promptly at 5:00, at which point a slightly cheesy recording of the national anthem is played, although the flag

---

[1]Other random jerseys, from real sports, spotted in the crowd: Chad Johnson, Jorge Posada, Calvin Johnson, Barry Sanders, Ronaldo, Drew Stanton (Lions), and Drew Stanton (Spartans).

seems to have been obscured by black draping that covers the entire upper rim of the arena so nobody really knows where to look. There can't be more than 2,500 people here, but the people that are here are enthusiastic and eating circus food, including cotton candy and flavored ice. In fact, for a moment, I feel as though I'm a kid again, at the circus with my parents. It's a good feeling. The fans seem to know all of the Raw stars, even the early-card guys like Santino, an Italian heel, and his opponent, a jheri-curled Mexican guy named Super Crazy.

"Super Crazy is a jobber," explains Vandermolen, "he always loses, but he does a lot of sweet moves." He's best known for moonsaulting off a balcony during an ECW show, and for a brief time holding a belt called the "ECW Television Title."

Santino Marella's schtick, meanwhile, seems to be saying a phrase or two in Italian, and then translating it to English. He takes the microphone before the match and engages in a few minutes worth of banter that riles up the crowd. I'm impressed by his professionalism on the mike. The Raw roster put on the exact same show last night in Kalamazoo and will be in Detroit tomorrow for a *Monday Night Raw* taping. The schedule alone must be exhausting, so to put on a physical show like this in front of a mostly empty arena on a non-television card is impressive. I'm also impressed by how into this I am. Before long I am chanting "let's go Super Crazy!" with J. R.

In between each match, a female WWE emcee rewards a lucky fan with the opportunity to come out of the stands and be a part of the show. One fan gets to ring the bell for a match, another, a middle-schoolaged girl, gets to be a valet for one of the matches. It's one of the flourishes that goes unnoticed on televised cards, but adds to the homey, family-friendliness of a live house show.

Next, there is a singles match pitting Hardcore Holly against a jobber whose name nobody catches. The jobber is a youngish, ripped white guy with a flowing mane of bleached-blonde hair. Even the jobber takes the mike and riles up the crowd, now eager to see him take a beating. "You people just don't know what it's like being a natural," he explains.

"You'll never make it in this business," screams the nine-year-old seated next to me. "I've been watching wrestling my entire life, since I was one year old," he says, "and I can tell you that this guy will never make it." He goes on to explain that his grandfather, also a wrestling fan, used to sit him on his lap as a baby to watch wrestling, and that his favorite wrestler is Jeff Hardy, who is "unfortunately suspended for doing the drugs." He says, "the drugs."

In the ring Holly, 45,[2] who is known for "stiff" wrestling and really breaking his neck in the ring in a very stiff match against Brock Lesnar, quickly dispatches the jobber. Holly returned to wrestling after surgery and a 13-month hiatus and has always been sort of a mid-card personality, though he now holds a share of the WWE World Tag Team Championship with Cody Rhodes.

Rhodes, meanwhile, wrestles the next match against a heel named Snitsky, whose main feature is that he's big and he apparently has bad teeth, according to the nine-year-old who, later in the match, will yell "brush your teeth!" to Snitsky, who will yell back "shut up, my teeth are fine!" This may be, in fact, the greatest moment of his nine years on earth, as he beams from ear to ear for the rest of the event.

Rhodes is, of course, the son of wrestling legend Dusty Rhodes. And while his father was known for being fat, sloppy, and "regular"—the blue-collar champion—Cody has a very fit physique. "His physique doesn't look unattainable," says J. R., while Vandermolen adds, "That's how I'm going to look after P90X.[3]" They're both delusional. They'll never look anything like Rhodes—though I feel a little gay for even writing this much about his physique.

Snitsky, whose real name is Gene Snitsky, is 6′8′′ and 307 pounds. He played offensive tackle for the University of Missouri, and is himself not young, at 38. Rhodes ends up beating Snitsky by way of a sloppy DDT, and the fans around me lament the fact that Rhodes doesn't have a real finisher—sometimes using the DDT, and at other times using a very ordinary "bulldog" to finish off opponents. What I also notice, though, is that the wrestlers continue to "sell" their in-ring injuries all the way up the tunnel that leads out of the arena. That is, if their left leg was wrenched in the ring during a match, they will limp on that leg for the rest of the night.

Perhaps the first real energy of the night comes from a tag-team match featuring Cryme Tyme. Cryme Tyme is an African American

---

[2]Watching an entire card like this, start to finish, gives a real perspective on how old many of these guys are. Triple H is 38, Shawn Michaels is 42, Kane is 41, and John Layfield is 41.

[3]P90X is one of those faddish workout regimens that can be ordered through late-night television.

tag team consisting of a character named JTG[4] (real name Jayson Paul) and Shad[5] (real name Shad Chad Javier Jesus Roman Chittick Gaspard). Cryme Tyme shimmy-shakes down to the ring to the beat of an indiscernible hip-hop tune. JTG is wearing a Kevlar, bullet-proof vest, while Shad wears a throwback Patrick Ewing jersey. They both sport an assortment of gangster-ish bandannas, ball caps, sagging pants, cornrows, tattoos, and other examples of thug-related symbolism.

The crowd loves Cryme Tyme. Even though they are portrayed as the kind of large black men who may in real life carry guns and steal your car, the mostly white crowd is eating up their schtick. And the African American fans in my section seem to have no problem with Cryme Tyme trading on negative ethnic stereotypes. The point here, I guess, is that you don't go to wrestling to solve social problems; you go to be entertained and have fun.

In real life, Shad Gaspard, from Brooklyn, was an accomplished No Holds Barred fighter and amateur boxer, and even played a little bit of college basketball. Irony noted, he also, according to Wikipedia,[6] "has been arrested numerous times, including arrests for assault in New York, New Jersey, Florida, Kentucky, Ohio, Georgia, Illinois, and California; looting and robbery in New York and Georgia; and drug-trafficking in Atlanta." Art, it seems, does imitate life. As part of their gimmick, Cryme Tyme regularly steals items from other wrestlers and then sells them to the crowd. This is either a brilliant example of wrestling and Vince McMahon having a sense of humor, or it is a giant step backward for civil rights.

Before the match, Cryme Tyme holds microphones hip-hop style, and leads the crowd in a chant that starts "Money, Money," (them) and ends "Ya! Ya!" (us). It's nonsensical, but fun, and speaks to the fact that wrestling superstars still appeal to fans on the basis of three basic desires—money, sex, and power.

---

[4]Formerly known as "The Neighborhoodie."

[5]Formerly known as the "Head Nigger in Charge."

[6]So this, of course, should be taken with the proverbial grain of salt—although, it also occurred to me that the WWE or Cryme Tyme could have updated their own Wikipedia page with this sort of information in order to build up the legend of Cryme Tyme by making you think that they are, in fact, authentic gangsters when, in fact, they may not be. I'm thinking about this way too much.

Their heel opponents are, brilliantly, a redneck tag team outfit consisting of Lance Cade and Trevor Murdoch (real name Trevor Rhodes, no relation to Cody Rhodes). Murdoch, sporting muttonchop sideburns and a cut-up flannel shirt, is as pasty, rural, and white as Cryme Tyme are urban and black. Though I would, carefully, categorize most of this audience as more like Trevor Murdoch than Shad, they clearly side with Cryme Tyme. Weird.

Most of the match involves JTG taking a beating at the hands of Trevor Murdoch, and then Shad tagging in to clean house. The highlight, though, comes when JTG, freshly launched out of the ring, staggers over to a white fan in the front row and takes a bite of popcorn out of his container. He then swigs from his soda cup as the crowd roars its approval and the fan beams as though he'd just won the lottery.

After falling at the hands of Cryme Tyme, Murdoch, after rolling around in the ring "selling" his pain for a while, takes the ring microphone and begins singing a surprisingly good rendition of the song "Friends in Low Places" by Garth Brooks which will always make me think of Blackford High School and the class of 1994. He gets almost to the end of the first stanza before having the microphone ripped from his hands by Cade, who shouts, "What are you so happy about? We just got beat!" Cade then storms from the ring, prompting Vandermolen to explain: "That's foreshadowing. There's been a rift between them for a long time."

****

Before the intermission, an emcee informs the crowd that they have the ability to choose the "stipulation" for the upcoming ECW title match between Kane and Chavo Guerrerro. By texting their preference—a "no disqualification match," or a "best-of-three-falls match"—to an announced number, the crowd can actually choose the "stipulation." This is another brilliant bit of marketing on the part of the WWE.

The show is a well-oiled machine. There is no lag time between matches and a constant buildup of energy toward the main event. Post intermission, there is a mostly nondescript "girl match" pitting current WWE girl champion Mickie James against a woman with a very square jaw named the Glamazon. We decide that girl matches exist mostly so that people can watch the bottoms of the girls in the girl matches, an attribute pro wrestling shares with women's beach volley-ball and sometimes gymnastics.

Guerrerro is booed heartily upon introduction, and looks even smaller than his 5′9′′ when faced with the 7′0′′ Kane (real name Glen Jacobs). Kane played college football and basketball at Northeast Missouri State, where he became the career leader for field goal percentage and led the team in rebounds and blocked shots per game in the late 1980s. For what seems like forever, Guerrerro slinks out of the ring and away from the advances of his much-larger opponent. This is the first time that my own endurance for the event has started to wane. I feel like getting through this match will be a struggle, but hope that the main event offers something interesting.

The nine-year-old next to me is chanting "Chavo sucks!" as if his young life depends on it. Most of the rest of the 2,500 or so people in attendance are doing the same thing. Though Guerrerro the professional must be pleased at his ability to generate that much heel "heat" from the audience, I also wonder what hearing your own name with the word "sucks" behind it, night in and night out, must do to a person's self-esteem.

As this is a "No Disqualification" match as stipulated by the fans, it is the only match of the evening that features a foreign object of any kind, and in this case, only a chair for a short time and then the ring microphone, which makes a satisfying thud when pounded onto the head of one of the wrestlers. This (no props) is refreshing. There are no tables being crashed through at ringside, and there is no blood anywhere on the entire card. Also refreshing. The wrestling is fast-paced, acrobatic, and relatively stiff, but I like the idea of not seeing people get maimed.

Kane eventually dispatches Chavo via a chokeslam, his signature move. As its name suggests, it involves grabbing someone around the neck, lifting them off the mat, and then slamming them down on their back. It's a great, visual finisher when you happen to also be 7 feet tall, like Kane.

After the Chavo/Kane match, the arena goes completely dark, as the crowd waits to see who will be participating in the main event. This, making the crowd wait to see who wrestles the feature, is an interesting and different wrinkle. In years past, fans could see a printed "card" with matches listed, which gave them a feel for who would be wrestling, but also locked the promoter into delivering those matches. This way, it builds a sense of anticipation, while also giving a promoter the flexibility to change the feature in case of injury, fatigue, etc.

****

It takes about two notes of their aforementioned clangy guitar riffs to alert the audience to the presence of D-generation X, also known as Shawn Michaels (also known as HBK or the Heartbreak Kid) and Triple H. As the two strut into the ring (Michaels limps, but more on that later) I feel the first surge of true celebrity excitement in the arena. The fans seem charged to be in the presence of these two wrestling legends, and I write that without the least hint of irony. They are both, in fact, legendary in the business—Michaels (real name Michael Shawn Hickenbottom) having held four world titles and Triple H (real name Paul Michael Levesque) with 12 titles to his credit.

As I mentioned before, Michaels has a significant limp on the way to the ring, as a result of an injury (kayfabe) he suffered in a previous match, as part of a previous storyline. When both men get to the ring, they stand on each set of turnbuckles to preen for that section of crowd, and Triple H does the patented thing where he spits a mouthful of water up in the air, not unlike a whale, and into the crowd. This is supposed to be exciting for those who get doused by his water/spit, and judging from the audience reaction it is, in fact, exciting.

My wife, upon seeing Michaels and H for the first time: "Do all of these old wrestlers have to grow long, skanky, stringy hair?"

Me: "Yes."

My wife: "What happens when they start going bald?"

Me: "They keep growing it anyway, see Hulk Hogan."

Michaels is unique in that he is of average size and looks to be one of the few WWE superstars that isn't roided up beyond belief. Still, he looks good, and he and Triple H enter into a vignette of crowd banter that they probably perform at every house show. They're both squatting, for some reason, as they talk into the microphones, and Triple H mentions something about the millions of fans watching worldwide. Michaels reminds him that it's a house show (laughter). They then give their signature line of dialogue: "If you're not down with it (crowd joins in, loudly), SUCK IT!"

This draws a roar of applause from those in attendance. I'm amazed at how much of the crowd chanting deals with sucking it, who sucks, or who the man is. I know I mentioned this before, but it's still noteworthy. Also noteworthy is the wrestlers' skill on the mike. In addition to being physically proficient, these guys have all managed to overcome a basic societal fear to become better-than-average public speakers.

Michaels's ethos, much like that of Edge as discussed earlier, deals with being an old man trapped in a young character. My first recollection of Michaels was back in the AWA days when he was tag partner with Marty Jannetty in an outfit called The Midnight Rockers. They wore lots of teal, and lots of little bandanas tied around their long hair, as well thighs, biceps, etc. This was when glam-metal was in its heyday, and everyone was trying to look like Motley Crue and Poison, and being a "rocker," especially a "Midnight Rocker" was very cool. Really not much has changed about the Michaels character since then, except that he's no longer young, and the pastel-colored spandex has been replaced by black-and-red leather pants. Still, he does a pretty good job of selling the "young" thing, as you don't, for the most part, feel like you're watching an older guy.

The house lights go down again, as John Bradshaw Layfield's (JBL) country music begins to play. Layfield, dressed in old-school wrestling trunks, a shiny nylon jacket (Mamajuana Energy, more info below), and a 10-gallon cowboy hat, makes his way down the runway, bathed in spotlight. His name sounded familiar to me, and it's because as a teenager I was a huge fan of an ill-fated spring football league called the World League of American Football. Layfield, at that time (1991) was recently out of college (Abilene Christian) and fresh off a short stint with the Los Angeles Raiders, and he played offensive left tackle for a team called the San Antonio Riders, which also included Dallas Cowboys offensive coordinator Jason Garrett.

JBL's gimmick is that of a glad-handing businessman, and that's where his story, for me, gets interesting; because in real life he is a glad-handing businessman. Layfield (in real life) is employed by a firm called Northeast Securities as a senior vice president. He discusses conservative political views on a nationally syndicated talk radio program, and he has a bestselling financial book on the shelves called, appropriately, *Have More Money Now: A Common-Sense Approach to Financial Management*. The book was published by World Wrestling Entertainment in 2003, and was described by one reviewer as "an endless parade of useless football and wrestling stories." The book is interesting, though, because despite the review, it does appear to have actual financial advice. But the fact that it was published by WWE makes me wonder if it isn't just another prop in the development of the Layfield character.

Layfield, a heel, looks the part of the rich, Texas a-hole. He has short, feathered blonde hair, and, in recent years as a wrestler, has become known for his ability to absorb savage beatings in the ring. His character has survived many iterations, however, as he spent time as a sort of identity-less Texas brawler named Bradshaw[7] with the obligatory stringy skank hair and a more roidish body, and before that as a character named Johnny Hawk.

JBL drew some real heel heat at a house show in Germany where, in an attempt to fire up the crowd, he gave a few Nazi salutes and goose-stepped around the ring. He defended his actions by saying, "I've done the Nazi salute for years," and "I've lived in Germany." His actions drew a typical, corporatized apology from CNBC, stating, "We find his behavior to be offensive, inappropriate and not befitting anyone associated with our network."[8] Though after he and the network made up, so to speak, they said "John brings a fresh perspective to the stock market, politics, and finance. We are excited that he is part of our team and look forward to his engaging, entertaining insights." Their only apparent stipulation, moving forward, was that Layfield avoid playing characters like "a stock market cheat, or a fraud." Currently, he describes his character as "a cross between J. R. Ewing and Pat Buchanan."

He heads a company (Layfield Energy) pushing a product called Mamajuana Energy[9] (Layfield pronounces it "mama-ju-wana") that he describes as "sex in a bottle,[10]" and "virility in a bottle." The compound, according to its Web site is, "an all-natural, non-alcoholic drink inspired by the Caribbean Legend, Mamajuana. Mamajuana Energy's

---

[7]This character used to actually "brand" his victims in the ring, using a branding iron dipped in ink, rather than the real kind.

[8]Is there anything better, or more unintentionally funny and meaningless, than the PR-department-produced corporate apology? This sort of thing happens all the time in real sports leagues like the NFL, NBA, and MLB and never ceases to come off as both unintentionally hilarious and completely shallow.

[9]Tagline: "Come to Mama for great sex."

[10]Layfield's father, Lavelle, is a minister.

proprietary formula contains a blend of herbal ingredients that boost energy as well as increase stamina and virility. The non-alcoholic 'shot' has a mixed-berry flavor and can be consumed straight or as a mixer." Mamajuana Energy retails at $42.95 for a 12-pack, and comes in a bottle that looks not unlike a tanning oil container. Its sister product is T-Shot Energy, "the first energy drink formulated specifically for golfers." Finally, an energy drink for golfers.

Layfield is fascinating, in part, because he's good at something else and doesn't need to be wrestling. He doesn't need to travel, at age 41, to a different town every night to be hit with chairs, thrown out of rings, and generally beaten upon. The thing is, he's great at it. He's great at generating heel heat, because the kind of people who watch wrestling generally hate the kind of people who are like John Layfield—bigger, richer, and better looking than them.

That said, he spends the greater part of the match taking a beating. His tag partner is Umaga, who is 35 years old and the nephew of legendary tag wrestlers Afa and Sika, better known as the Wild Samoans. Umaga looks like a wild Samoan himself, covered nearly head to toe in tattoos, and sporting a weird cornrowish configuration in his hair. He also wrestles barefooted. Umaga is himself a huge guy, going 6′4″ and 350 pounds.

The Umaga/JBL pairing is one of the odd tag teams that happen in wrestling, when there is no natural tag partner available for a given superstar. The JBL and Umaga characters have nothing really in common, save for the fact that they're both heels, and you get the feeling that they exist just to give popular tag teams like DX someone to pound on.

Though Michaels and H are the bankable stars, the real energy in this match comes from Layfield—partly, as I mentioned before, because he doesn't look or usually act the part of the mulletted, spandexed pro wrestler. The match ends with Layfield taking a series of Sweet Chin Musics from Michaels, and then getting pinned. He lays in the ring after the match, for what seems like forever, and then, very slowly, gets up and staggers down the runway, selling his pain by pirouetting and falling occasionally, as though concussed. The crowd loves this.

Michaels and Triple H, meanwhile, circle the arena, glad-handing audience members for a good 20 minutes, posing for pictures, signing autographs, and generally making people feel great. This is unique in that it would never happen at an NFL or NBA game.

****

The arena empties around 7:20, a tidy two hours and 20 minutes after the opening bell. The rain has stopped, and it's still light outside. Everyone is smiling, and nobody is drunk. There's something to be said, I think, for early start times, as people generally behave better in the daytime. There's something about a veil of darkness that seems to give a person license to be an idiot.

CHAPTER 10

Wrestling Isn't Fun (or Why I Started the Literary Wrestling Alliance)

I want a lot out of life, and I want a lot out of my audience.

—Iggy Pop, rock star

LWA (THE LITERARY WRESTLING ALLIANCE)

Mission: A federated alliance of Montessori-trained wrestlers/writers/visionaries endeavoring to combine the pageantry and athleticism of wrestling with the excitement of live literary events. And when I say Montessori, I mean that all of our wrestlers are self-trained by either watching lots of videos or working with each other. And when I say literary, I mean that we all love books and there will be live readings of poetry, short fiction, and literary nonfiction between matches at our events. We will also strive to provide pizza and pop free of charge.

Upcoming Event: The Literary Wrestling Alliance will disband immediately after one show in the Spring/Summer of 2008. The show will include the following:

- A Haiku Match, where in order to win, the wrestler must climb a ladder in the middle of the ring and write a haiku containing five, seven, and five syllables. The Haiku will then be read aloud.

- A Postmodern Lit Match where there is no winner or loser, but the wrestlers will just stop wrestling when they feel like it and the audience will decide the winner based on applause.
- Literary Readings from Each Wrestler.
- T-Shirts for Sale.
- Free Pizza and Pop (aforementioned).
- A Short Wrestling Clinic. Conducted by Ted Kluck, this will give audience members the opportunity to learn a few minutes' worth of real wrestling knowledge.
- A Tag Match.
- A Singles Match.

****

This afternoon I spoke with the self-proclaimed (from its Web site) "Kingpin"[1] of an organization called "Prime Time Wrestling." I called something called the "PTW Hotline," which was really this guy's cellular phone. I got a garbled "hello" when I dialed the number, and asked about press credentials for an upcoming event featuring former WWE star Sid Vicious.[2] What I should have realized before I called is, there's no such thing as press credentials for wrestling events. I'm used to the NFL and NBA, where you have to fax reams of paperwork from your publisher, your blood type, FBI fingerprinting, and the like just to apply for a credential. Conversely, in boxing, they will give a press credential to anyone, for any reason. I have sat at ringside next to correspondents working for internationally published glossies, who are sitting next to pimply 16-year-olds writing for their high school newspapers. In wrestling, there's no such thing as the real media, so there's no such thing as real credentials.

Another e-mail exchange with WWE public relations chief Joe Villa further illustrates this point. Villa, for the record, was more than

---

[1]Does anyone really refer to himself as "a Kingpin?" This strikes me as especially odd/sad, even in the odd/sad world of professional wrestling, where this type of thing is fairly commonplace.

[2]This is, of course, the 6′9″, 317-pound wrestler, and not the former Sex Pistol. It is interesting, though, how much wrestling borrows so many of its storylines and characters from stuff that happens in real life. For what it's worth, his real name is Sid Eudy, and he's from Arkansas.

helpful, and even very pleasant. However, he shared with me the fact that the WWE has its own publishing arm,[3] which means that its current stars are all unavailable for interviews from now through the duration of their contracts. Ditto, I assume, for the old geezers (Hogan et al.) who are all probably still under personal services contracts with the WWE (i.e., show up and make an appearance a couple of times per year). This bit of news was a blow, to say the least, and will make it very difficult for me to do part of what I had hoped to do with this book, which was interview old wrestlers.

The only thing I can compare this to is the media lockdown that was a part of Cold War–era Soviet states, where the government controlled television, radio, and print. Even in leagues that are relentlessly image-conscious (the NFL, for example) players can still pretty much act as free agents when it comes to giving interviews. That said, though, this makes all the sense in the world for the WWE, as it allows them to control the message and the medium to the extent that their wrestlers are saying what they want them to say, and when and how they want them to say it.

****

Starting my own wrestling federation is more work than I expected. Our struggles at the moment include finding a ring, after a local boxing/martial arts studio fell through. Our one workable venue seems to be a popular barn/party spot on the outskirts of Lansing. There is also the job of finding wrestlers with dual passions for books and wrestling. I targeted several potential workers and sent them the following letter:

Gentlemen,

Consider this your first official correspondence from the Literary Wrestling Alliance, billed as "the greatest one-night spectacle of literary and wrestling talent ever assembled."
Some LWA projects in the works:

---

[3]This publishing arm has been responsible for an awful spate of wrestler biographies, perhaps best illustrated by Hulk Hogan's book *Hollywood Hulk Hogan*, which I'm really ashamed to say that I read in its entirety even though I knew throughout that much of what I was reading was a "work." I mean, this book really sucked. For what it's worth, Mick Foley has written great books, and Chris Jericho's book *A Lion's Tale: Around the World in Spandex* is pretty good too.

—A magazine. We're going to pattern our mag after the crappily-done wrestling mags of the 1980's . . . poor quality photos, newsprint pages, etc.
—Promos. We'll meet at Vandermolen's place sometime soon to "cut promos"—which means shooting the little videos where we yell about what we're going to do to each other.
—T-Shirts. I can design/sell these through my website.

As for the event itself, we're going to have a bunch of concept matches involving literary stuff:

> *—a haiku ladder match, where the winner has to climb a ladder and write a haiku*
>
> *—a hardcore match involving old laptops and used books*
>
> *—a "Publishers Weekly" review match*
>
> *—a Battle Royal*
>
> *—an Old School chain/mat match.*

That said, we don't have a date or a ring yet, but we're working on those things. Drop me a note back and let me know your availability in mid-late July. I'm working a couple of contacts, including a local boxing promoter, on securing a ring, and we're in preliminary discussions about the Pollitz Barn as a potential venue.

Also, be thinking about your characters, and whether you'll be a face or a heel.

Best,
The Great American Author (face), Ted Kluck

As a result of the letter, our roster is rounding into form, including the following:

- Butthole Nick Vandermolen (heel)
- The Righteous Warrior, J. R. Grulke (face)
- Evan "Plagiarism" Chisolm (heel)
- The Irresistible Force, Patrick Kelly (face)
- Nasty Charlie McMasters (heel)

Perhaps most disturbing is that most of these guys had thought about their ring names and angles without me even asking.

Our little federation comes of age, officially, at Vandermolen's apartment, as we hash out storylines and cut our first promos. Vandermolen has taken on the task of crafting a storyline, as he is currently applying for similar jobs with the WWE. He lays out his vision for a show in which a NWO-ish heel organization, called "Publishers Weekly,"[4] does battle with a group of faces, including yours truly. The main event of the evening will be the Haiku ladder match pitting Vandermolen against me. The idea is that I'm injured in the opening battle royal, but rally for an inspirational victory, and then vanquish Vandermolen in the haiku match at the end. However, the wrinkle comes when I then join forces with Publishers Weekly, which represents the ultimate in betrayal for a real writer.

The storyline set, Evan begins setting up a camera to shoot some promos. The idea being that we'll eventually post them on our various blogs and Web sites to "promote" the show. However, the real idea behind this is that they're just a lot of fun to do. Randy Savage was legendary for his hilarious promos. Ditto for The Ultimate Warrior, whose promos were nonsensical but nonetheless perfect for his sort of unhinged, perhaps-insane character. Researching bits for my own promo, I came across this Ultimate Warrior classic:

> I was in the castle from a place long from here and I came here for one reason to attack and keep comin' not to ask but just to give not to want but just to send, send the power of the warrior down everybody's throat in the wwf til they become stick of it, well your gonna get sick of it because this freak of nature right here is just beginning to swell and when I get big enough brother their aint gonna be room for any body else but me and all the warriors floatn' through the veins and the power (uhhh) the warrior.

I move a huge pile of junk out from Vandermolen's bookshelf, in front of which I've decided to shoot my promo, in keeping with the Great American Author theme. His apartment is a mess. His buddy J. R. recently married, and the apartment has since devolved

---

[4]As an author, I have a latent distrust for all book critics, even, for some reason, the ones who like my books. So it is intuitive that our heel outfit be named for the group of critics that routinely trashes almost every new book on the market.

completely into what seems like a giant pile of dirty clothes, at the center of which is a television with a Wii, an Xbox, and a stack of wrestling videos including new ones on Triple H and the Hardys. I pull a coffee table away from the bookshelf, upon which is the emptied-out hull of an old computer (which we'll use in our Publishers Weekly hardcore match) and a copy of my last book, *Why We're Not Emergent* on top of a copy of Paris Hilton's book entitled *Confessions of an Heiress.*

I don a sportcoat and light a pipe for my promo, in which I accuse Nick Vandermolen of being "nothing but a critic." I read from the actual PW trashing of my second book, *Paper Tiger,* for inspiration. And then I slowly remove the sportcoat, flex, and ask Vandermolen "what are you gonna do, when the Great American Author runs wild on you?" It's ridiculous. All the while he sits off camera, serious, stroking his chin not unlike a Hollywood film director. He then pulls a pack of cigarettes out of the freezer (why?) and shows me the future of cigarettes ("they're smokeless"). He puts one behind his ear and one in his mouth to begin shooting his own promo, but after a few dry minutes in front of the camera, chickens out. "I've gotta think about this some more."

"What should we call our show?" Vandermolen asks, as the meeting breaks up. Wrestling events always have testosterone-friendly names like Fully Loaded, Bad Blood, One Night Stand, Armageddon, and No Mercy. We kick literary names around for a little bit, such as "First Edition" and "For Whom the Bell Tolls," though nothing sticks. Finally, I suggest "Pride and Prejudice," which we all agree upon, if for no other reason than it might persuade girls to come to the show who may end up dating Jarmo or Vandermolen.

After the meeting breaks up, the recently married J. R. and I hang around, chatting, long into the evening. Most of the guys are nearing graduation, and Vandermolen is planning a move to Chicago. A common conversational thread, lately, has been "what's going to happen when Vandermolen leaves?" I opine that many of us will quit watching wrestling.

"I came into Vandermolen's apartment on a Monday night, freshman year," J. R. remembers, "and he was watching *Raw.* I immediately said 'this is stupid, we haven't watched this since middle school.' But it sucked me in and we've watched it together every Monday night for five years. But after Vandermolen leaves in the fall, and after you're done with the book, I doubt I'll watch it or talk about it again."

****

NICK VANDERMOLEN'S LWA MAGAZINE BIOGRAPHY WRITTEN BY NICK VANDERMOLEN (REPRINTED WITH PERMISSION OF LWA MAGAZINE, VOLUME 1, ISSUE 1 AND NICK VANDERMOLEN)

Name: Nick "The Critic" Vandermolen

Height: 5 7

Weight: 190

Real Name: Nicholas A. Vandermolen

DOB: 8/7/85

Hometown: Alpena, MI

Other Names: Butthole, El Dangeroso (his masked persona)

Finisher: The Black Lung (Modified Wheelbarrow Sit-down Facebuster)

Submission Finisher: The Red-Eye, Lombardo Armbar (Tag-team finisher with his tag team Lombardo Barnyard)

Signature Moves: The Bad Review (Stylized Electric Chair), Cocky Pin, Cigarette Stomp (Modified Orton Stomp), The Fault Finder (Inverted Headlock backbreaker), Back Rake, Fist to the Junk, Eye Poke, The Seventh Chakra Technique (w/ Lombardo Barnyard)

Quotes:
"When I'm on stage, it's my time."
"It's not about who wins. It's about who dies."

Highest Rank on the LWA top 100: #2 (July 2008)

Championships and Accomplishments:
BWA Tag-Team Championship—with Nick Jarmo (2005) (1 time)

Favorite Books: Lombardo Barnyard: Year 1, Lombardo Barnyard: Level Up, Michigan Mythos: Series 1, Michigan Mythos: Series 2, http//turnyour computeroff.blogspot.com

---

All the wrestlers of LWA know that to get to the top, they're going to have to go through Nick "The Critic" Vandermolen. This rule-breaking, cigarette-smoking madman is notorious for giving bad reviews in and out of the ring. A critic of both the literary world and the wrestling world, his hands/pen has ended and created the careers of many superstars, most notably Nick Jarmo.

Jarmo and Vandermolen burst onto the wrestling scene in late 2004 with their tag team Lombardo Barnyard. These two friends met while training at Alpena's prestigious Basement. After graduating from the Basement, this tag team quickly made their presence known at the BWA (Basement Wrestling of Alpena) by using highly innovative offense. With signature moves like the Lombardo Armbar and the seventh chakra technique, these two babyfaces were not only dismantling opponents, but breaking their will to live. After bulldozing though BWA's mid-card tag-team division, Lombardo Barnyard was clearly the number-one contender for tag-team gold. It was then that Lombardo Barnyard entered into their first extended program with Brent Champagne and Simon Jack, the BWA tag-team champs at the time. After a series of false finishes and run-ins by other BWA superstars, Lombardo Barnyard challenged Brent and Simon to a series of "Basement Destroyer" matches to settle which tag team was really the best in BWA. These matches were so hard core and so extreme that the Lombardo Barnyard "best of" DVD had to be severely edited to meet DVD morality standards. The rivalry escalated into the infamous Weapon Wall Basement Destroyer Match at BWA's last pay-per-view, Kill the Basement. Bamboo, TVs, knives, stacks of out-of-date dictionaries—nothing was off limits for these four competitors. Despite Vandermolen suffering from a broken rib he got from Kevin Bush's five-star frog splash in a singles match a week earlier, Lombardo Barnyard won the ultraviolent match. But, the commissioner of the BWA, Tim Vandermolen, ordered a stop to these ultraviolent matches because they were too dangerous. He was too late; the Michigan Board of Health deemed BWA too violent for their "great northern state," and subsequently BWA was shut down forever.

Vandermolen, Jarmo, Brent Champagne, and Simon Jack put their differences aside and joined the then-steadily growing promotion AAW (Alpena Area Wrestling). The four, having gone through some of their toughest battles together, became friends and started a heel stable known as the Pipe Crew. The Pipe Crew quickly made a name for themselves as the NWO of the north. They consistently interfered in matches, and routinely cheated. Although they vied for the top, they were never able to make more than a few ripples in the AAW. Many diehard fans of the stable still exist. Seeing more opportunity in the south, Jarmo and Vandermolen moved to SCF Wrestling. SCF Wrestling focused more on traditional grappling and wrestling, rather than the hard-core wrestling style Vandermolen and Jarmo were used to. Rule breaking was highly reprimanded at SCF Wrestling. Vandermolen and Jarmo once again reformed their tag team Lombardo Barnyard and, with the BWA belts still in hand, quickly challenged the SCF Wrestling tag-team champs Evan Chisholm and Alex Meyer for a belt unification match. The winner of the match would unify both belts and become the unified SCF Wrestling tagteam champs. At "Fall Retreat," one of SCF Wrestling's biggest pay-per-views, Lombardo Barnyard lost their BWA belts to Evan and Alex in an anticlimatic "falls count anywhere" match. Training in the hard-core style for so long, Lombardo Barnyard was not able to overcome the technical prowess of Evan and Alex. Lombardo Barnyard floundered in SCF Wrestling for another year until taking some time off to write.

Lombardo Barnyard focused on their writing career and were able to find success in there first novel, *Lombardo Barnyard: Year 1*. This nearly 300-page book featured writings on how to become tag-team champs, as well as their story on how they became the stars they knew they were. While on a tour of their book, Vandermolen began writing *Michigan Mythos: Series 1* and *Series 2*. Jarmo opposed the Michigan Mythos series because of their insensitivity and negative attitude toward many of the Michigan wrestling promotions. This caused tension for the two in and out the ring.

In 2006, Lombardo Barnyard reformed in the AAW, but tension between the two was too great, and they quickly broke apart. Jarmo turned face and vowed to overcome the evil of Vandermolen's pen. Jarmo called Vandermolen's writing "bad to the bone," and "black as night." This led to another extended feud that fueled the careers of both men. Their grudge matches were brutal and violent, but Vandermolen had a tendency to run from the fight when he started to lose. To counteract Vandermolen's cowardice, Jarmo created the rope battle. The pinnacle of the feud, the rope battle consisted of a six-foot rope, each end tied to the each wrestler's right foot; the object of this dangerous match was to strangle the person with the rope that was tied to their foot. After a series of dangerous spots, Vandermolen tapped out and left the AAW arena a bloody mess. He never returned to AAW again.

Weeks later, fans found Vandermolen in the LWF (Lowebrook Wrestling Federation). He had many highly praised feuds with Pat

Kelly and J. R. Grulke. These battles helped LWF become a top promotion in the area and helped Vandermolen become a top heel in the territory. Despite Vandermolen's success, he was never able to obtain the LWF gold. In 2007, the commissioner of the LWF, Lynzo, changed the name of LWF from Lowebrook Wrestling Federation to the Lynzo Wrestling Federation and changed the name of the LWF championship belt to the J. R. Championship belt, which was held by J. R. Grulke at the time. Vandermolen and J. R. feuded for the J. R. Championship belt for months, culminating in an interpromotional show at the pay-per-view *SCF Talent Show*. After a hard-fought battle, Vandermolen once again lost and left the promotion to continue with his writing career.

While away from wrestling, Vandermolen joined *Publishers Weekly* and began critiquing the writing of many wrestlers. He critiqued none more harshly then the Great American Author Ted Kluck. Every week Vandermolen would publish a review berating the writings of Kluck, calling him "a has-been" and "an old man trying to relive his glory days." During this time, Vandermolen began work on *Lombardo Barnyard: Level Up*, a book full of stories that were too explicit for *Lombardo Barnyard: Year 1*. Jarmo caught wind of the new Lombardo Barnyard book, and challenged Vandermolen to a Lombardo Barnyard death match. The winner would get the rights of the name Lombardo Barnyard, Jarmo said, "Anywhere, anytime, any promotion." Vandermolen responded by saying, "It's not about who wins, it's about who dies." Kluck, GM of the LWA, wanting to also get his hands on Vandermolen, invited him and Jarmo to the LWA to have their death match at LWA's first pay-per-view, *LWA presents Pride and Prejudice*, on August 1.

At the contract signing, Ted Kluck issued a "No touch" clause, which stated that if Vandermolen and Jarmo fight, in any promotion before August 1, the match is cancelled. It's been hard for both Vandermolen and Jarmo, their bad blood for each other boiling over, but they wait patiently wrestling matches at LWA waiting to get their hands on each other. All the while, The Great American Author Ted Kluck watches over, waiting to get his own hands on Nick "the Critic" Vandermolen.

CHAPTER 11

The One about Christian Cage (PCW's Dream Night 7)

I like Christian Cage almost immediately. His DVD intro is uniquely hilarious. Unique, because he eschews the traditional wrestling clichés of highlights, explosions, and testosterone-driven, screamy rock music. Instead, Cage compares himself to a number of societal innovations, including the Model T, space travel, the hula hoop, and sliced bread, and then explains why he eclipses them all and is the champion of the universe. It supports my original thesis, which is that wrestling, to really work, needs to kind of make fun of itself.

What makes the DVD great is that Cage himself is really nothing to look at. He's the guy at your local Gold's Gym with the goatee and the spandex shorts, which could describe every guy at your local Gold's Gym. He's fit but not unnaturally, roidily huge. He's a good athlete, but not the best athlete. He's a high-flyer, but not the highest flyer. He has charisma, but not the most charisma. That's what makes his DVD—complete with footage of Marilyn Monroe and the Space Shuttle—so funny and cool. The DVD release is billed as "the biggest in wrestling history," except that everyone knows that's not true. In fact, TNA (Total Nonstop Action, Cage's current employer) might be out of business by the time it actually releases.

Cage is from Kitchener, Ontario, and, like many Canadians, shows a healthy capacity for self-deprecating humor despite his decorated wrestling career. He debuted in 1995 and has since held European, Intercontinental, Hardcore and tag titles (WWE) in addition to the TNA heavyweight title (twice). He is perhaps best known for the WWE tag belts he won with his kayfabe brother and real-life best friend Edge. Supposedly, the WWE offered to re-up his contract, but he declined, citing frustration over what he perceived to be disproportionate screen time for Triple H as well as seedy storylines.

Once again, I'm taking in this show with my cousin Brian, who has been an on-again, off-again fan of wrestling. "In your mid-twenties there are only a select few people to whom you can admit to liking wrestling," he explains. "When I worked at the railroad, I would make fun of guys mercilessly for liking wrestling. There were a lot of guys walking around in Stone Cold Steve Austin T-shirts." Tonight he's dressed in jeans, black work boots, and a NOFX T-shirt. He has a scummy ponytail and facial hair, and looking around the room it dawns on him that, at some level, he looks like much of the crowd. "It's really time for me to change my look," he deadpans. In this crowd, everybody is trying very hard to be unique, and in doing so, nobody is actually unique. "The most rebellious guy in the room tonight would be the guy in khakis and a golf shirt," Brian opines. "And that guy is you." I'm guilty as charged.

It's an hour and a half until bell time and the wrestlers are going over spots in the ring. They include a doughy black guy in a full Penny Hardaway Orlando Magic uniform circa 1992. I run into "Whiplash," who got married recently and is eating from a bag of McDonald's fast food an hour before his match. His fiancée became Mrs. Whiplash two weeks ago as evidenced by her T-shirt, which says "Mrs. Whiplash" across the back. "Now Wally Wylde is my brother-in-law," he says, "so when I call him brother,[1] it's really true now."

Around the room there are the obligatory merchandise tables,[2] concession area, and an area in which fans can pay $20 apiece for an autographed 8 x 10 of Christian Cage and Sunny Sytch, who is here on a return engagement.

---

[1] In wrestling, you'll notice that everybody calls everybody "brother," which is probably a holdover from the Hulk Hogan era where he called everybody "brother." It's eerily similar to some church traditions, where congregants regularly refer to each other as "brother."
[2] Featuring an all-new "No Blood, No Fun" Butcher T-shirt.

"I get all of that," says Rick Jenig, as if reading my mind. "And if those seats fill up, I'm a wealthy man," he adds, pointing to a stack of folding chairs in the back. For a relatively small appearance fee,[3] Jenig can sell pizza, T-shirts, and tickets at $10 for the cheap seats and $20 at ringside. He's selling fans on the opportunity to be close to a real, live famous person, and by all appearances, they are buying. They charge through the gates when they open at 6:05.

The event is taking place in a community gymnasium called the Oak Lawn Pavilion, and my seat is somewhere near the top of the basketball key. There are signs up advertising adult volleyball, and a dirty sheet of paper asking patrons not to spit on the jogging track. I see two five-year-olds in front of me drinking Mountain Dew, and I realize I would rather let my five-year-old son play with oily rags or razor blades than willingly give him Mountain Dew in the evening. There are several adults carrying those plastic, toy WWE championship belts. There is a local X-Sport fitness table that is empty, while a comic book shop has a table next to it that is thriving. I get depressed and walk to the table to buy an official PL Myers "Chicago Connection" T-shirt. I feel like I shouldn't like overpaying for this merchandise, but I do. The truth is, I like the PCW, I like Meyers, and I like Rick Jenig. This is good, weird fun.

Meyers is in the room now, his ear glued to a cell phone. His modus operandi seems to be "walk around and look important." He walks in little circles,[4] talking into his phone. "Let me know if you need anything," he says, between calls, which I know means "I hope you don't actually need anything because I'm very busy." I mention something about an interview with Cage. He mentions something about not being able to clear it with TNA, which would have been a convenient conversation to have, say, a few weeks ago.

Jenig won't be wrestling tonight, unfortunately, as he tore a muscle in his lower back doing "the same morning workout I've done for the last 20 years." He is the most "together" or normal-looking person here. He's a businessman who also happens to love wrestling. I'm bummed I won't get to see him work tonight. He paces the room nervously, watching the room fill up, and directing his grade-schoolaged nephews, both of whom clearly worship the ground he walks on. They

---

[3]Two thousand dollars for Cage, and $800 for Sytch.
[4]People either pace in straight lines or walk in circles on phones. Meyers is a circler.

look exactly like him, right down to the long blonde hair and glasses. This makes me smile.

****

One of the more interesting things about Christian Cage is his age. He's 35, which is right around the age most wrestlers disappear or push through to become lifers (such as Shawn Michaels, Triple H, Ric Flair, and a bunch of other old wrestlers). At 35, he seems for some reason to be the wrong age for "Dream Night" or any other indie show appearance, for that matter. In Dream Nights past, Jenig has hosted older wrestlers like Bret Hart, but it seems like, at 35, Cage should have something better to do, though I'm not sure what that something would be.[5]

According to PL Myers, Cage has the "it factor" and has come to represent a sort of perfect scenario for the promotion. In earlier Dream Nights, they would commission two huge-named wrestlers to come in and have a sort of dream match, though such an endeavor would now cost, according to Meyers, "at least 10 grand." But Meyers says, and I agree, that fans want instead to have a "defining moment" with the visiting wrestlers, which is another way to say it's more satisfying to shake Cage's hand and get his autograph than it is to see him wrestle. This is not an indictment of his wrestling; it's more just a commentary on how people like to interact with celebrities. Meyers then tells me a story about waiting in a line for hours to shake the hand of current prosperity-gospel proponent Joel Osteen, who was in Chicago doing a book signing and service at the United Center. Osteen is a traveling televangelist and pastor of Lakewood Church in Texas, which is so big that it meets in an old NBA basketball arena. Meyers waited in the line, and spent roughly two seconds with Osteen, who he then discerned was "a really down-to-earth guy." This, I think, is the point of events like this, and the reason that fans drive from "five states away" to see Cage. They want to be with a famous person, and share that famous person's space and oxygen for a while, and then be able to make a pronouncement about that character like "he was really cool" or "he was a dick." It doesn't really matter if that famous person is a televangelist

---

[5]Probably spending time with a wife and kids, but that's also probably just me superimposing my own standards onto Cage. But come to think of it, I'm also here without my wife and kids.

telling you to follow your dreams, or a pro wrestler telling you to follow your dreams.

"Chicago doesn't really have a wrestling legacy," Meyers[6] explains later. "We're not like Minnesota, or the East Coast, or Texas in that we had our own territory. Chicago fans are fickle, but we want to give them opportunities to meet some of these guys in person. Meeting Bret Hart (a former PCW Dream Night guest) is a once-in-a-lifetime opportunity. What's more special? Seeing a guy wrestle, or being able to have him sign your first wrestling magazine and thank him?"

Cage takes the microphone shortly after the first match,[7] and it's soon apparent that because of the acoustics in the room, it will be impossible to hear anything he's actually saying. Cage is dressed in jeans, a black T-shirt, and a black baseball cap, and looks very ordinary physique-wise. He's not a huge guy. He's not even a big guy. From the top of the key (Cage is probably at midcourt) he looks like he weighs about 195. Though I can't understand him, Cage is good-natured on the microphone. He says something about the White Sox, and this being the South Side, everyone cheers. He brings out a guy from the crowd who stands 6′11″ and makes much of his height.

I know from television and the videos that Cage is really good on the mike. He has a higher-pitched voice, but like most successful wrestlers, he has a gift for improvisation, which makes him stand out amongst the forest of personality-challenged, roidy giants like Batista. Shortly after he joined TNA, Cage made an impassioned in-ring speech about why he left WWE. In addition to not-so-subtle barbs in the direction of Triple H (something to the effect of being tired of seeing the same guys give the same speeches every night), he goes on to express his love of wrestling, in a speech that seemed more shoot than work. It occurs to me that perhaps the fans like Cage because he truly

---

[6]Kudos to Meyers here for maintaining kayfabe through the majority of our interviews, in the sense that he never told me what his real job was, rather, insisting that he works full time for PCW, which I know is not true.

[7]This was a great tag match featuring Whiplash and Wally Wylde in action against a couple of sinister-looking "Chicago Connection" heels. It's taken two shows, but I've really grown to appreciate the Wally Wylde character—a hard-partying, fat, frat-boy type in board shorts, with leis around his neck. Wylde is consistently hilarious, the fans love him, and he's a better-than-average wrestler. In fact, of all the PCW wrestlers, he's the one who I think has a real chance at climbing the ladder, even though his physique is less than spectacular.

likes their "thing," even though he's cool and talented enough to like something else.

What's odd, though, is what happens when Cage exits the ring. He's mobbed. Like it was when the Beatles were mobbed. He exits on the opposite side of the ring from where I'm seated (thank God) and I can see a mass of black T-shirts and bad skin flowing toward him, and security guards running after to try to subdue the throng. I truly didn't expect this. Granted, I don't expect people to just sit impassively in their seats, but the scope of his celebrity here is impressive and unexpected to me.

Marshall McLuhan once said that the medium is the message. That quote has occurred to me often during this project. Is Christian Cage still Christian Cage without the aggrandizing effect of television, which makes everything and everybody appear larger than life? I would have said no, but the crowd's reaction makes me think otherwise. There's something happening here, and what it is isn't exactly clear to me at the moment.

****

It would be wrong of me, in the midst of doing perhaps the single dumbest thing I've ever done—trying to create a wrestling federation for one night only, for the purposes of this book—to suggest the wrestling here at Dream Night isn't good. On the contrary, it is quite good. They do everything here—ladder matches, busted tables, high flyers, etc.—that they do on television, and they generally do it really well. Television just adds a layer of removal (again, the media being the message), so it's easier to willingly suspend disbelief. What they're doing here will be eons ahead of anything we're able to accomplish.

As for our little group, we take in the matches much like one would take in a baseball game. They are happening in the background, we glance toward them occasionally, and then we resume talking. We discuss the movie *The Darjeeling Limited*. We lament the fact that there are very few good comedies anymore, while a few feet away from us, a man (Steve Heisman) fails to crash through a table when slammed upon it. The irony escapes us at the moment. How we can fail to be entertained by a man crashing through a table is beyond us all.

We watch my old trainer Jay Phoenix wrestle a great match against the one man on the card who seems to have the "standard" wrestler look—a guy named Steve Boz, who is shaved, tanned, and tweezed and has the kind of long, bleachy 80s rocker hair one would expect of a professional wrestler. Phoenix is a great wrestler as well and pulls off a variety of big moves that you wouldn't expect from a guy who weighs upwards of 250 pounds. He's a tremendous athlete. Boz seems obsessed with making his pecs "bounce"—which if you're a guy who grew up watching wrestling in the 80s, or you're a guy who's ever looked at himself in a mirror, I don't have to explain what that means. Come to think of it, if you're neither of those things, you're probably not reading this book.

There is a match in which Fusion, the nice guy in the Lucha mask from my training session, wrestles to a draw because the time limit (10 minutes) expires, which never happens. He hits a memorable leg drop onto his opponent, who is also on the ring apron, off of which they tumble onto the concrete floor. We all wince because it looks real.

After the Phoenix match, we go outside, where one cigarette turns into three or four, and we spend time discussing the fact that Gramps only got mad at us when we screamed like we were hurt, but that wrestlers scream like they're hurt all the time. Then we both decide we're starving and leave to get a burrito across the street, thankful for Rick Jenig and Pro Championship Wrestling for making these meetings possible.

CHAPTER 12

The LWA Presents Pride and Prejudice Continued (or, the End of the Matter)

When I was a child, I talked like a child, I thought like a child, and I reasoned like a child. When I became a man, I put childish things behind me.

—1 Corinthians 13:11

I'm not exactly sure how I came to build a wrestling ring in my basement, but I do know I'm standing in a local tire place asking the hungover kid behind the counter for his discarded tires.

"What do you need them for?" he asks. A fair question, to be sure.

"I'm building a boxing ring in my basement," I reply, as though this is the most normal thing in the world. The truth is, I've lost sleep over it. I wake up in the middle of the night thinking about plywood, turnbuckles, and ring ropes. I've used the word "taut" more in the last week than I have in my whole life, to this point. Attaining rope tautness has become something of an obsession, and not an entirely healthy one.

The kid goes in back and in a few minutes produces an armload of tires. In fact, he encourages me to take as many as I need. I've got my buddy J. R. with me, and we load the dirty black tires into the back of my car, giddy as schoolchildren. The tires will sit beneath the plywood and provide "bounce" to the ring. I found the plans on the Internet, which is more proof that you can find nearly anything online.

"Good job telling him that this was for a boxing ring," J. R. says as we drive away. "It sounds more reputable."

****

I've never built anything with my hands, so this ring represents a sort of Mount Everest for me. After a very expensive trip to Lowe's, we return with a truckload of lumber, carefully placing it in my basement through an open window. For an OCD neat-freak like me, a pile of lumber in the basement is a huge problem. I ask my friends to continue to remind me that this was a good idea, because I'm feeling a lot like it's the dumbest thing I've ever done.

Surprisingly, framing the ring is much easier than I thought. Vandermolen and I throw in a Rob Van Dam DVD in the basement player, and set about our work. We have only the most rudimentary of tools —two handsaws, a hammer, and an assortment of screwdrivers. I look over at Vandermolen once, and he looks like a caveman hacking away at a piece of wood, hair flying in all directions. I can tell that Vandermolen has never built anything in his life, either, so between us, we seem to have the knowledge and ability of one below-average man. This is less than encouraging.

As an aside, I've been trying to "sell" Vandermolen to one of my publishers, in hopes of getting him a job upon graduation. He has a phone interview in a week, and I hope beyond hope that he won't tell them about this project, both for his own good and for mine.

Soon, the pile of lumber has turned into a ring frame—four posts and sidewalls. My wife has been an angel through this. She wakes up with me in the night to tell me that the ring will be fine. She even walks down to the basement to admire my work periodically.

****

LWA EXCLUSIVE: AN IN-DEPTH INTERVIEW WITH THE GREAT AMERICAN AUTHOR, TED KLUCK (REPRINTED WITH PERMISSION OF LWA MAGAZINE, VOLUME 1, ISSUE 1)

Name: The Great American Author Ted Kluck

Height: 6 '2"

Weight: 220

DOB: 3/15/76

Hometown: Hartford City, Indiana

Other Names: James Dean, Holden Caulfield, David St. Hubbins, Richie Tennenbaum

Signature Moves: The Holding Caulfield (Von Raschke Claw), The Tenure Track (Choke Slam), The Needle in the Hay (modified gut-poke), Ibid (DDT), The Shark Sandwich (bear hug).

Titles Held: AWA, NWA, WWE, IRS, ATF, CIA, DEA, NASA, UNICEF, NATO, SAG, WGA, and NAFTA

Interview:

AM: What's a young, talented, world-famous author doing in professional wrestling?

TK: Dave Eggers is wrestling, too?

AM: No, you.

TK: Of course. (Lights pipe.)

AM: You've had a well-publicized feud with Nick Vandermolen, a critic at *Publishers Weekly*, even going so far in an interview with the *New York Times*, to call him, quote, "a pathetic little weasel of a man" and, quote, "a joke of a writer who should look forward to a satisfying career writing for Guideposts," end quote.

TK: I'm not proud of that interview, though I stand by it.

AM: You're a highly successful and, I might add, awfully attractive young writer. You won the Heisman Trophy as a college football player, you've been internationally recognized for your humanitarian work, and you're a better-than-average Hollywood actor. Why the anger?

TK: Nick Vandermolen hasn't written a positive review since 1985, and he personally trashed my award-winning second title, *Paper Tiger*. I once saw Nick Vandermolen tell a classroom full of small children that they should quit writing immediately and instead study small appliance repair. What I've never told anyone, publicly, is that I was in that classroom that day.

AM: You were one of those small children? Were you crying?

TK: Yes, and yes.

AM: Would you say a bit of your innocence died that day?

TK: I would.

AM: After a better-than-average NFL football career, a star turn in several warmly received independent films, and a brief career as a literature professor, you turned to pro wrestling, winning titles in the AWA, NWA,

WWE, IRS, ATF, CIA, DEA, NASA, UNICEF, NATO, and NAFTA. What's left to accomplish?

TK: I've never won a haiku ladder match. And I've never had a *New York Times* bestseller.

AM: Your books have always struck me as more thoughtful, erudite, funny, and deep than most of the pap on the *New York Times* Bestsellers list.

TK: How sweet of you to say. (Smiling.)

AM: Would you say you're on a collision course with Butthole Nick Vandermolen?

TK: I wouldn't have chosen those words, exactly, but yes, I would say that. (Removes sportcoat, flexes.)

****

Charlie McMasters and Evan Chisolm wrestled in high school, which is readily apparent as soon as they get into the ring in my basement. They know what they're doing, and I gain a whole new respect for what can be picked up, pro wrestling–wise, via a high school wrestling background and an insane amount of time spent watching tapes and episodes of *Raw*. These guys are good. Better than two-thirds of my class at Price of Glory.

Vandermolen and I look at each other with looks that express something like: "Our match is going to suck by comparison, but that's entirely okay." Vandermolen has printed agendas for the evening (our first, and probably last, practice) that say things like "items that need to be taken care of: merch table, VIP bracelets (?), miscellaneous."

"I really like projects like this," he explains, stating the obvious. "I like to put all of my promotional skills into practice." I'm not sure to what promotional skills he's referring, but I know that this will be his last project in East Lansing, as he'll be moving to Chicago two days after our show. He has agreed to take on the rest of the magazine project, and we spend much of the evening getting posed and action shots for the mag, which will then turn into fake reports on dark matches, contract signings, etc. Vandermolen and I pose, eyeball to eyeball, in front of a bookcase in my office, in the classic "press conference" shot. He sits at my desk and pretends to sign a LWA contract.

His Butthole Nick Vandermolen character is rounding into form nicely. He wears a torn denim jacket into the ring with jeans (also torn), and a black do-rag headband. For all his bravado, Vandermolen expresses trepidation at ad-libbing the match. "I'd like to script every-thing," he explains. We then begin to walk through a litany of moves that we'll be comfortable doing to each other, in a makeshift ring that's holding up remarkably well, considering. I hip toss Vandermolen, I bodyslam him, and then we run ropes. Finally, I choke slam him by putting my right hand around his doughy, bearded neck, and appearing to lift him up with one hand while he jumps and take a back bump. Shockingly, the move looks cool, and is easy.

****

NOTES (SCRIPT) FOR MY MATCH WITH VANDERMOLEN

I. Intros
–Nick leaves ring continually, refusing to wrestle.
–Several lockups/breakups/Nick heeling
–Kluck wins test of strength, after which Vandermolen leaves ring.
–Finally, we chain to the atomic drop by Ted.

II. Babyface Shine
–Kluck lands series of kicks and chops.
–Toe kick and Vandermolen feeds into a Bodyslam.
–Elbow drop to back.
–VM leaves ring to recover . . . Kluck turns back to sign autographs . . .

III. Heel Shine
–VM hits double axe handle to Kluck's back . . .
–VM hits series of knee-drop type moves . . .
–VM tangles Kluck in ropes, hits chops . . .
–VM turns to play to crowd while Kluck recovers . . .

IV. Babyface Finish
–VM tries series of clotheslines . . . thwarted twice.
–Kluck hits clothesline on third attempt.
–Kluck gets ladder into ring . . .
–Hits chokeslam #1 (no ladder)
–Hits chokeslam #2 (with ladder)
Kluck writes Haiku (end of match)

****

EVENT NIGHT: THE LWA PRESENTS PRIDE AND PREJUDICE

My basement has rounded into form nicely. One of my goals for the evening was to make sure nobody who actually knew about wrestling could be invited to the event, so that there would be no real criticism. That plan was foiled, however, by Juan, who looks like he bench-presses Buicks, works with Evan Chisolm for an outfit called "Tunes by T," and is here to run the sound system. Juan shows up about a half-hour before opening bell, and is introduced into a whirl of activity, including popping flashbulbs, posed photographs, magazine distribution, and a microphone check in-ring. I can tell that Juan, who has wrestled in indie and backyard shows on and off, is impressed. Everything we've done here was done to create the illusion of legitimacy—which, come to think of it, pretty well captures the whole spirit of professional wrestling.

"We go big here at the LWA Juan," I tell him, between sitting for a portrait and running a plate of cookies from my kitchen down to the assembled crowd. I start to explain to Juan that everything here at the LWA was done somewhat ironically—that we basically started the promotion so that we could design T-shirts and make a magazine. I explain to Juan that my match, the main event, will be "like a Hogan match . . . maybe eight minutes, tops." In fact, much of what we've done with the space (basement) and presentation of the evening is meant to deflect attention from the actual wrestling.

Juan will be seated behind a stack of amplifiers and a sound board.[1] Vandermolen has placed a pile of 20 8 x 10s on each seat in the basement, "so that fans can get autographs after the matches." The 8 x 10s, which are actually 8.5 x 11 sheets of copy paper, feature all of us in various training maneuvers and poses, and the collective effect of these papers strewn all over my basement is one of a copy machine explosion.

****

AN ASIDE ON MY RING WALK MUSIC, AND HOW SWEET IT IS

For a wrestler, choosing ring-walk music is probably the most important thing in one's repertoire, besides maybe "gear" (a.k.a.

---

[1]Special thanks to my good friend Tom Gheen here, who goes big in everything he does. Tom provided the amps and microphone, and offered a fog machine (declined) as well.

clothing). As we all learned in high school music classes, music conveys emotion and stirs reactions in people; therefore, it's important for a babyface to pick babyfaceish music,[2] and for a heel to pick heely music. For example, Vandermolen (heel) chose a song by Motorhead called *Ace of Spades*, and the Publishers Weekly heel stable will all walk to the ring to *Ice, Ice Baby* by Vanilla Ice—a double-entendre meant to play upon the fact that Ice plagiarized most of that song from a song by David Bowie.

But enough about their music. I chose "The Warrior" by Patty Smyth and Scandal, which I would characterize as upbeat, guitar-and-drums chick rock in which Smyth sings about "shooting at the walls of heartache," whatever that means. "The Warrior" is the kind of song that worms its way into your subconscious, causing you to involuntarily hum or whistle it at random times. It is also quintessentially 80s and almost always makes the listener feel good, making it the perfect wrestling babyface song. At the risk of patting myself on the back, I received compliments on it all night.

****

ANOTHER ASIDE ON THE PHILOSOPHY BEHIND YOUNG PEOPLE AND EXCESSIVE PHOTOGRAPH TAKING

I am the oldest wrestler in the Literary Wrestling Alliance by a good decade. I'm 32, and the rest of the workers have either just graduated from college or are on the verge of doing so. That said, we have vastly different philosophies vis'a vis photo taking/archiving. Simply put, these kids take a ton of photos. They photograph almost everything they do from nearly every conceivable angle for the purpose of then publishing all of the photos via Facebook[TM] or Myspace[TM]. So much so that actually doing the event (a wrestling show) takes a backseat to photographing and archiving the event. This is either a really cool way to archive the events in one's life, or proof of a rampant narcissism that will eventually be part of our downfall and destruction as a society. Either way, this explains why the two most competent people in my basement on the night of August 1 are photographers.

---

[2]See also, the section on Hulk Hogan and his "I Am a Real American" theme song, which sucked but was oddly catchy and played upon the idea that Americans are good and everyone else is bad, which is exactly the idea that all of wrestling played upon throughout most of the 80s.

Jim Olson, a doctor by trade and a photographer by hobby, is a friend and a very good photographer. His friend, Michael Chen, is even more into photography. The following is is an incomplete list of all the stuff that Michael brought into my basement, for the sole purpose of photographing the wrestling show:

Giant blue backgrounds.

Metal clamps (for hanging the backgrounds).

Strobes (i.e., flashy lights that make a picture look sweeter).

An extension cord.

A spring-loaded silver thing that looks like a cross between a futuristic umbrella and one of those portable partitions that women dressed behind in old movies. This, also, has something to do with lighting, but I'm not sure what.

Lots of lenses.

Because Jim took pictures for my arena football book, I know he understands me and my sense of humor. I'm not so sure about Michael, however, and am worried that he's not "getting" the whole pro wrestling thing—though I'm worried, at times, that I don't "get" it myself. However, as the night progresses, Michael seems to be having a wonderful time, and tells me as much at the end.

****

Ten minutes before bell[3] time, we encounter our first major problem of the evening. Paladin (J. R. Grulke) is screwing around in the ring, attempting a hurricane-rana[4] on Butthole Nick Vandermolen. This is a spot they were going to try in the Battle Royale, but instead Paladin's feet get tangled in the ropes, and both mens' bodies pull down hard on the top rope, snapping a screw that attaches the ring post to the base of the ring.

It goes without saying that the wrestlers shouldn't even be in the ring at this point, much less working through spots while the crowd is trickling in. I point to the drill and a box of screws and go upstairs to find my wife before I kill J. R. and Vandermolen for real. Training has been a nail-biter for me, for this reason. I knew we had a strong

---

[3]We had to download a ringside bell sound from an Internet Web site a few minutes before bell time, as we had all forgotten this very important detail up to that point.

[4]I don't really know how to describe this, except that it's a flippy thing off the top rope that involves scissoring your legs around the other guy's head and then taking him down.

ring, but each training session tested it to the max. If I were a betting man, I would have guessed that it would have been Evan and Charlie who would have destroyed the ring, enamored as they were with corner moves. We postpone the start of the event by 15 minutes, as my friend Tom, who is handy with all things construction-oriented, fixes the ring.

Regarding the crowd,[5] I'm shocked that people have actually shown up for this. We invited only a select number of friends, billing it as an "exclusive" event that will be a cross between a wrestling show, a literary event, and a typical Kluck house party. They seem to be milling around comfortably, flipping through the magazine and wondering about the pile of 8 x 10s on their seats, one of which seems to feature Vandermolen hitting a crab pose in his underwear.

The ring disaster averted, I gather the wrestlers in my office for a short meeting and prayer. Two of them are wearing face-paint, and Vandermolen has ripped his Publishers Weekly[6] heel stable T-shirt to reveal a pudgy, pale abdomen. Charlie looks like a little, Asian superhero[7] in red tights and a red Under Armour shirt. Surreal doesn't begin to describe the atmosphere.

We make our way to the staging area (also the bottom of the basement stairwell) and I walk the ring to "The Warrior." Then, oddly, the event comes off generally just like we planned it. Our friend Stefan (a girl) sits in the back row with a horrified look on her face the whole night. My very intentionally indie friend Steve is equally mortified in the front row during the battle royal. We all walk and pose our way into the ring, Vandermolen flipping empty cigarette tubes at the fans, and Evan stealing the show by swinging into the ring via a ceiling rafter. I bodyslam and then choke slam J. R. to win the battle royal in quick and efficient fashion.

---

[5]If Internet photographs are any indication, we seem to have outdrawn many of Michigan's independent wrestling promotions; most of which struggle to fill a handful of folding chairs at ringside. This, of course, is less a testament to our wrestling skills, and more a result of really loyal friends.

[6]This is a good time to apologize/explain to those in the employ of *Publishers Weekly*. We did name our heel stable after your publication, because you did trash my second book, *Paper Tiger*. But no hard feelings, seriously, and it has all worked out really nicely for our storyline.

[7]His finisher: The Asian InvAsian.

Vandermolen is then summoned back into the ring for a reading from his second book, *Lombardo Barnyard Volume 2: Level Up.*[8] Except that he doesn't read from the text at all, rather, he just talks about how much Jarmo sucks and heels it up before their Lombardo Barnyard Death Match. Heeling it up, Vandermolen makes like he's going to high-five my son Tristan in the front row, pulling his hand away at the last minute. A few moments later Tristan is crying (not because of that, rather, because he has to go to bed), and Vandermolen spends the rest of the night asking me if Tristan is okay, which is really thoughtful.

Jarmo's match with Vandermolen is a marathon of groin shots and outside-the-ring pandemonium. It tests our audience's endurance while also ending up being something of a dance of friendship between these two best friends who will part ways soon. Jarmo will stay in town to finish a criminal justice degree, and Vandermolen will move to an undisclosed location in Chicago to do an undisclosed (read: as yet ungotten) job. Jarmo's character can best be described as a mix between John Adams (the former president) and a country farmer on steroids. He walks to the ring waving an ancient American flag that he'll later use to bludgeon Vandermolen's crotch. His finisher is called the Continental Congress, and is a series of groin shots.[9]

To be honest, this is the match about which I'm most nervous. I've spent the preceding week pleading with both guys to not kill each other in the ring, saying very dad-like things like "your health is the most important thing." I know they'll push the envelope, which is why I have trouble watching. At one point, Jarmo throws a stack of books at Vandermolen's face, one by one. I exhale and breathe a sigh of relief at the end of their match, when they both stagger down the aisle, selling. They're both recounting details of their match before they even get to me, which is another one of the reasons people do things like wrestling. Much of the joy comes in the retelling.

There are odd, little juxtapositions all over the room. Competing with the rock music coming out of the amps, there is a baby monitor

---

[8]Lots of people ask me what this book is about, and the best explanation is that it's about Nick Jarmo and Nick Vandermolen, but it manages to not be one of those self-indulgent, narrative nonfiction, "my life is so hard" sort of books. It's really just a collection of their stories, which end up being surprisingly funny and likeable even for people other than their friends and families.

[9]Also known as reasons I put Tristan to bed early.

plugged into the basement wall, out of which we can hear the crying of Stefan and Josh's new baby. Directly adjacent to the ring is a large, white box containing Kristin's wedding dress. A sacred memory from a sacred day. Now there's a wrestling ring in our basement.

Next, it's Evan and Charlie, the two high school wrestlers who have the best chance at putting on a good wrestling show in the ring. They don't disappoint. Theirs is a fast-paced, ECW-style match filled with lots of flipping around and dropkicks. It's better than a large percentage of indie-show matches I've seen this year, and I hope I'm not just saying that because they're my friends. After Charlie's victory, Evan pounds him in the ring with a crutch, thereby setting up the showdown between Vandermolen and me in the haiku ladder match.

Again, the stipulation is that in order to win the match, the winner must climb a two-step stepladder and then write a haiku (five, seven, and then five syllables) onto a clipboard taped into the rafters. To my knowledge, this is a completely original storyline/gimmick. Before the match, I take the microphone and explain to the audience that Vandermolen is the critic from PW who trashed my second book, which isn't entirely true.[10] I explain that I am there for revenge, and that Vandermolen will pay, tonight, for the bad review. I explain that I will then retire, win or lose, after the match, from professional wrestling. Vandermolen then goads me into a pose-down, which we milk for laughs in much the same way that Will Ferrell parlays his soft, white body into laughs on screen.

Our match is also something of a goodbye. I met Vandermolen at church about a year ago, and we bonded over our shared fascination with wrestling. In a way, this show, and this match, was inevitable. We chain into an atomic drop, after which I can tell that Vandermolen is going to wrestle the match of his young life. He jumps high into the atomic drop, holding for a second at the top. It's a big move.

The match progresses, with Nick leaving the ring periodically to heel to the crowd, and me hitting a series of big moves, including a choke slam, after which the crowd begins to chant, "Ladder!" I grab the ladder and climb slowly, in true wrestling style, up the two steps, grabbing the clipboard at the top. Vandermolen then pulls me down, hitting me with the ladder for good measure. I roll out of the ring and

---

[10]Though *Publishers Weekly* did trash my second book, Vandermolen did not write the review.

onto the VIP sofa next to Linzo, where I claim that I'm too tired to go on and announce my retirement. At this, the crowd goes nuts and urges me back into the ring. I'm tired. This fake fighting is much more tiring than it looks on television, though I can see that the crowd is really urging me back into the ring, meaning that they're not just being nice; rather, they're into the storyline. For the first time, I feel like we've actually succeeded.

I roll under the bottom rope and climb back into the ring. Vandermolen is up on the ladder, writing the second line of the haiku. It's important that I don't pull him down before the second line is written. I feel like the crowd is in a throaty roar at this point, but I may very well be imagining that. I punch Nick in his doughy abdomen, and then grab him around the neck for a huge, final choke slam off the ladder, which he lands perfectly. He's now nearly dead in the center of the ring. I pull the clipboard down and write the last few words of poem with my foot planted on his chest. From my vantage point in the ring I can see almost the entire audience, and all of them are smiling.

****

There's a random assortment of people still sitting around my living room, rehashing the event. Jim Olson, the local physician and photographer, and his wife Jenny, age 50. There are Josh and Stefan Hull, and their newborn baby. J. R. (Paladin) and Linzo. Everybody is reliving the event. I still have my "gear" on, that is, the cutoff "Ted Wins" T-shirt and jeans. I'm sweaty. It's weird to be here, doing this.

Jarmo leaves almost immediately, packing up his American flag and wearing his gear—cutoff shorts, cutoff shirt, cowboy hat—out into the Grand Ledge night. Vandermolen is still somewhere in the basement; perhaps still in the ring. It was his idea to stage an "autograph signing and book sale" after the event, and through the floorboards and open basement door, I occasionally hear him yelling, "Signing and selling over here!" though I don't think he's signed, or sold, much of anything. At one point, our friend Stefan asks, "Is he as crazy as he seems to be?" I reply that indeed he is, and that he is also a very good, albeit raw, writer. Vandermolen is the type of guy who will be famous one day, largely because he's relentless, and he's willing to take things much farther than most other people.

He comes up the basement steps, arms loaded down with extra magazines and copies of *Lombardo Barnyard Volume 2: Level Up*. On top of the stack is a crude spreadsheet, outlining his sales figures for the evening. Vandermolen is not unlike the Dignan character in the Wes Anderson film *Bottle Rocket*. He does his planning and organizing in very unorthodox, childlike (but effective-seeming) ways. Seeing the magazines reminds me that in many ways, we started the federation just so that we could make the magazines. It was a tail-wagging-dog sort of proposition that ended in what I'm confident is the greatest independent wrestling mag/program ever conceived and executed. Vandermolen will save every excess copy, and they will all go in a file marked "LWA Mags" somewhere in his apartment.

Before he leaves, I tell him that I'll visit him often in Chicago. "You've always got a place to stay," he replies, though I know that he hasn't yet secured a place to stay for himself. I give Nick a big hug on the way out. After all of my worry about starting the federation, building the ring, and putting on the show, now, I have an empty ring in my basement and I begin, distinctly, to miss wrestling.

EPILOGUE 1

Josh Abercrombie (Raymond), Dan Severn, and the Price of Glory

There looks to be about 30 people in the room, give or take the microphone guy, and the audiovisual guy, who looks like all audiovisual guys everywhere look. There is the usual independent wrestling assortment of ambiguously aged post-high-school small-town girls, (none of whom look like they actually want to be there, and most of whom are chewing gum) and their boyfriends. And old people. There are always old people.

The room, in this case, is the Price of Glory training facility, where I trained for the early part of this book, and which now presents a show called *The Judge, Jury & C. J. Otis*. More importantly, for me, is the fact that I'll be able to see many of the guys I trained with and under work on this show—Josh Abercrombie, who now goes by the name Josh Raymond, Louis Kendrick, Money Mike, Brian Skyline, and Jack Verville, the Grand Valley State linguistics major whose parents are, I'm pretty sure, sitting in the row of folding chairs behind my row of folding chairs. I can tell they're his parents because they look like him and they look too unbelievably normal[1] to be here. It occurs to me to turn around and offer a word of condolence or encouragement, but I can't think of exactly what to say, so I say nothing.

---

[1] They look like the kind of normal, affluent west Michigan parents who would have a kid in college, studying linguistics.

The main thing that strikes me about this scene is the silence. We're in a small room—in fact, my folding chair is set up over the mat upon which I learned to take my first bumps as a wrestler. The ring is lit by four bare light bulbs covered by one of those metal cagey-things that covered the lights in your high school gym class. You can hear the guys' boots shuffle along the canvas. You can hear them breathing heavily upon exertion in the ring. You can hear random people having random conversation in the crowd. My cell phone buzzes once, and I'm pretty sure one of the wrestlers looks in my direction. Somebody has their newborn baby here, and the baby cries once in a while.

In the ring is former UFC and WWF/E legend Dan "The Beast" Severn, in whose outbuilding this whole affair is housed. His ring is adjacent to his office, which is adjacent to his house. Severn had some legendary fights in his UFC career with the likes of Ken Shamrock and Royce (pronounced "Hoyce") Gracie. I'm pretty sure he's just doing this for fun, and hits about a million suplexes on an opponent named Keith "Shamrock" who is really the wrestler Keith Crème but is, for this, posing as a nephew of the great Ken Shamrock. He goads Severn for his older age, and makes a "Depends" joke before winning by disqualification after Severn gets caught by the referee with a chair in the ring.

Severn wrestled professionally in the NWA, where he was a world champion, and the WWF/E for two years, but is best known for being a Mixed Martial Arts icon. As research for this project, I watched a video compilation of Severn's MMA fights, many of which involved him getting his opponent on the ground and then kneeing that opponent in the head as many times as possible. This is an interesting way to make a living, to say the least. Severn, though, was one of the first high-profile amateur wrestlers to parlay that experience in the octagon. He was an All-American wrestler at Arizona State, originally, before starring in the UFC and professional wrestling circuits, and eventually making his way back here, to Price of Glory, where he's wrestling in front of maybe 30 people and appears to be having a blast.

Between the Severn match and the match featuring my old training partner Jack Verville, I notice the following:

- Every independent wrestling crowd includes one guy yelling vaguely homoerotic stuff. This never ceases to be weird.

- There are at least two wrestlers, so far, who wore the type of silver necklaces that were cool in 1997.
- There is a little girl sitting in the corner by the ring wearing pink pajama pants. My guess is that she's about five years old.
- Fake sweat, or bodybuilding oil, looks weird up close.
- I'm pretty sure some of these guys stuff their trunks à la the Shakespearean codpiece.

Jack is wrestling against a guy named Steve Amani, who seems to have a sort of rock star persona going, which means that he has silver trunks and wore sunglasses into the ring. Jack, a babyface, comes into the ring wearing baby-blue trunks, white boots and flowing blonde hair. He also seems to have brought a contingent of college girls with him, who are seated with his family in the row behind me. It's always easy to pick college girls out in a crowd like this. They squeal and giggle for real anytime Jack either does anything spectacular or appears to get hurt in the ring. Jack's parents say nothing and leave after his match, though it should be noted that they are smiling and wearing the expressions of proud parents. They are also wearing the expressions of people who are happy to be getting the hell out of the particular outbuilding they're in. It should also be noted that Jack wrestles a great match, culminated by a huge missed move off the top rope that appears to have really hurt him.

Next, a non-title tag match features a Jack Black-ian character called "The Hype" Jimmy Shalwin. Shalwin reminds me of Jack Black because he's fat, bearded, and smart. In fact, all of the wrestlers here tend to have pretty smart wrestler-to-crowd banter going, as evidenced by my old training partner Louis Kendrick's bit in which he plays a martial arts expert teaching the crowd how to tie their shoes. He ties the shoes while also making exaggerating martial arts screamy noises[2] and is interrupted in the ring by a guy named "The Old Timer" Jeff King, who I happen to know is a local insurance salesman when not wearing a one-piece singlet and old tube socks into the ring. King's gimmick is that he speaks in a growly, raspy voice like old-time wrestlers, which is funny because he, himself, looks like a pretty average small guy. King accuses Louis of being the illegitimate child of President Barack Obama, to whom he bears a striking resemblance.

---

[2]It occurs to me while typing this that maybe you had to be there.

I'm also struck by Louis's proficiency on the microphone, as I remember him being a mostly quiet, inward type of guy. Ditto for Jack, who seems to have lost his shyness.

Other things I notice throughout the course of the evening:

- One of the wrestlers uses the word "insipid" during his match. He also compares himself to the biblical character Lazarus, whom Jesus raised from the dead.

- Price of Glory spent a lot of money on cardboard tickets bearing the image of main event wrestler C. J. Otis, which I doubt they've recouped, based on the crowd.

- One of the wrestlers, Dollar, walks to the ring by a German rock song which says "Du Hast,"[3] which I'm pretty sure means something sinister in German, and which I'm also pretty sure was sung by the German band Rammstein,[4] though I will be too lazy to look either thing up when I get home.

- Many of the fans leave immediately after the matches that involve their friends or family members. This provides the reverse effect of the crowd getting progressively smaller leading up to the "Main Event."

I have absolutely no idea what to do during the intermission, so I wander back to the canteen area to mill around back there until the matches start again. I run into Mark Pennington, who is watching his preschool-aged daughters, one of whom was the mysterious girl in the pink jammie pants. They're sitting at a table and coloring. It occurs to me that of all of the independent wrestling shows I've experienced through the course of this project, this one is truly the most "family friendly," though they all claim to be. There hasn't been a drop of blood spilled at this show, and there have been no "gimmick" matches or foreign objects of any kind. No dog collars, thumbtacks, barbed wire, two-by-fours, or tables. This is refreshing. There has been no profanity from the wrestlers.

After the intermission, the microphone guy gets in the ring and promotes a future show called "Season's Beatings" which I think is the greatest name for a holiday show I've ever heard. It elicits a chuckle from the handful of us left in the folding chairs. Speaking of, there's

---

[3]My wife studied German in college and tells me that Du Hast, means "You have." Bummer.

[4]It is by Rammstein, and I did look it up.

a really old lady in a walker who's trying to leave, but she's timed it such that she might run into one of the wrestlers as he makes his way down the aisle. I'm not making this up, and this scenario provides some of the best drama of the evening. The rest of the crowd goes silent, rooting for this osteoporotic woman to make it to the door in time.

Every independent promotion has a Jewish wrestler named "The Hebrew Hammer." POG's Hebrew Hammer is a part of a tag outfit called "The Kosher Club," which marches to the ring in yarmulkes, slacks and vests to traditional Jewish music.[5] These guys use terms like "schmuck" and "the other day when I was talking with a friend over a good bagel." It occurs to me that this group may have been the slightly nerdy/funny/smart group of kids in high school that always wanted to do athletic things but never got the opportunity, then. They wrestle a great match against my other former trainer Brian Skyline and his tag partner Idol Heinze. For the most part, in terms of pure wrestling and wrestler/crowd interaction, this is the best show I've seen, top to bottom.

At this point, I notice the children in the crowd who are getting progressively more aggressive as the night wears on. They're up out of their seats, pretending to beat one another, just like their heroes in the ring. I begin to question the sanity of the parents in the room. It also occurs to me that I'm having real fun here. For perhaps the first time in the life of this project, I'm not checking my watch and/or feeling depressed because I've just seen a grown man blade himself. The show is fast-paced, clean, and entertaining.

Josh's main event match with C. J. Otis doesn't disappoint. Abercrombie does a good bit of flying around, crashing to the mats outside the ring on several occasions. He wears a sleeve over his right elbow, upon which Otis will work throughout the duration of the match—pain that Josh does an admirable job of "selling." Otis has worked extensively in Japan, and Josh is headed there shortly, where he hopes to make more money while experiencing Japanese culture. "I'm a big fan of Japanese culture," he explains, before telling me that this show is his third of the weekend. "The usual," he says. On Saturday night, he bladed his forehead, which left "a little gig mark right up by the

---

[5]It's at this point that a 60-year-old Midwestern woman stands up and begins dancing to their ringwalk music.

hairline." He was also involved in a storyline which had him licking the belly of a pregnant woman. All in a week's work.

Abercrombie works the remaining crowd into a frenzy, with smart, heelish dialogue that both makes the crowd love him and hate him. Or love hating him. Either way, it's effective, and he works this crowd as though there are 10,000 of them filling an arena. Otis, the blonde babyface, is a perfect foil. He's one of Michigan's top independent wrestlers, and, the last I heard, works at a grocery store in South Lansing when he isn't flying around in rings all over the state. His workouts here at the POG school are legendary. These guys have both worked in this promotion for a long time, and may continue working here for a long time, in front of 30 or so people. Or they'll end up in the WWE. Either way, I think, they're enjoying themselves, which, at the end of the day, is what makes people do this sort of thing. It's no different than guys playing semipro football on the weekends.

Driving home, I'm reminded of Harley, the sixtysomething-year-old who trained in my class once in a while. He intervened in the tag match tonight, as manager of The Kosher Club, and was carrying a scepter and wearing a yarmulke of his own. Harley has survived heart attacks and health problems of various kinds. He has fallen from high places and survived, as a working man. There are many ways to grow old, and tonight, waving his scepter and going nuts in the ring, he appeared to be having the time of his life.

Epilogue 2

Wrestling Magazines

I'm back in my cousin's old room, which is where I always stay when I travel to the Chicago area. On the tail end of this project, I'm looking forward to forgetting about wrestling for another decade or so, until my son is into it. I've had my fill, and if you get your fill of something, it may be proof that you never really loved it anyway.

Regardless, I'm drawn again to the stack of wrestling magazines on Brian's dresser. There are hundreds of them there. Seedy, colorfully tacky covers, cheap newsprint pages, and lots and lots of mullets. Sometimes the wrestlers on the covers are bloody. Other times they are triumphantly hoisting belts. Most of the "interviews" and "journalism" contained on these pages are "works"—which is to say that they are fake. Probably the writer both asking and answering his own questions. *Pro Wrestling Illustrated. Inside Wrestling. The Wrestler. Superstar Wrestler.*

One thing these magazines share in common is the nature of their advertisements: "Too Skinny—A New Shape in 30 Days!"[1] "Safe Acne Treatment!"[2] "Strong Arms Make All the Difference! Muscle

---

[1] Via one-a-day "Hercuplan" tablets. I'm not making that name up.
[2] According to the blurb, and an accompanying scary illustration, this is something called "Bio Masque," which is made out of salicylic acid and goes over your head. It looks horribly uncomfortable and more than a little dangerous.

Mix."[3] "Be a Locksmith!"[4] "Explosive Power in Your Hands and Arms with 'Hammer Fist.'"[5] "Pellet Firing Rifle with Scope."[6]

It's as though I'm seeing the suckiness of these magazines for the first time, and realizing, again for the first time, what the collective body of advertisements says about their readership: That you're an unemployed loser with bad skin, skinny arms, and no job, who desperately needs a pellet gun that looks just like a real gun. In *The Wrestler*, there's a columnist named Matt Brock who is photographed wearing one of those clear plastic visors you wear playing cards, smoking a cigarette, with a tumbler of hard liquor in front of him, next to a typewriter. This is the "hardened journalist" shot. It's great. Even the writers are workers.

It's past midnight, but I read an article on Andre the Giant about "The Tragedy of Success." I read about Robert Gibson, Ricky Morton, and "The Rock and Roll Revival." "The Hart Foundation vs. The Rougeaus." "Is Randy Savage Facing a Conspiracy?" I read about whether Misty Blue Simmes can save women's wrestling[7] and Bobby Heenan's bitter crusade to destroy Hulk Hogan.

There's a full-page advertisement and order form for what's billed as the "first LP" by Michael Hayes and the Badstreet Band, entitled "Off the Streets." The record company is called, ironically, Grand Theft Productions which (grand theft) is what was, I'm sure, perpetrated on the suckers who spent $9.95 on this famously bad album. The cover, though, is priceless. It features a bearded, slightly overweight Hayes shirtless, in a black leather jacket sporting a mullet of epic, bleach-blonde, hair-deadening proportions. This could very well be the mullet to end all mullets. Shockingly, the ad also offers something called "Michael Hayes 'Exposed,'" which they bill as an "un-retouched color photo, free in albums only!" Each chest hair rendered in painstaking detail.

---

[3]The most reputable looking of all the ads, Muscle Mix still boasts average "Gridth" (*sic*) increases of 2.84 inches.

[4]And earn up to $26 per hour after Foley-Belsaw's "shortcut training."

[5]Illustration: A guy with huge forearms smashing some wood with what looks like a giant hammer head strapped to his wrist. This product promises "sledge-hammer striking power and strength."

[6]And a carrying handle for "combat situations."

[7]The answer, clearly, was no.

In Brian's blue WWF duffel bag, I find our old cardboard belt — the one we wore on the videos we made in the ring we built out of old mattresses and garden hoses. The videos that were intended for our eyes only. It strikes me that there are probably stacks of magazines like this in childhood bedrooms all across the country. There are probably old VHS tapes labeled "wrestling" that contain these ridiculous, innocent memories.

I put the belt around my waist and look in the mirror, realizing that a lot of our childhood remains in this room, but that tomorrow is an early morning, and there's a lot of work yet to be done.

Appendix

Josh Abercrombie's Guide to Wrestling Terminology

Abortion	Failed match or angle.
Angle	Event or series of events used for a wrestling storyline.
Babyface/Baby/ Face	Hero; protagonist; good guy.
Blade/Gig/Geek/ Juice	To self-inflict a cut that bleeds.
Blade/Gig	Object used to self-inflict a cut.
Blown Up	Exhausted; gassed.
Book	To schedule a wrestler for a show.
Booker/Pencil	Person who books wrestlers.
Botch	Mess up. (Botched Spot = Blown Spot)
Boys	The wrestlers.
Broadway	A draw.
Bump	Fall.
Bury	(1) To defame or criticize someone. (2) To lower someone in the eyes of the fans.
The Business	The professional wrestling industry.
Call a Match	To inform opponent of upcoming moves or spots throughout the match.
Card	The lineup of the matches.

Carney	The secret carnival language spoken by wrestlers.
Carry	To lead an inexperienced wrestler in the ring.
Cheap Heat	Heat a heel gets by swearing, insults, etc. (which is easy).
Color/Juice/Red	Blood.
Comeback	A point in the match where the babyface comes back from the beating and turns the match around in his favor.
Cut a Promo	(1) To do an interview. (2) To demean someone skillfully.
Cut-off	A point in a match where a heel cuts a babyface off.
Dagger	A blade/gig with more of the razor exposed than necessary.
Doing Business on the Way Out	Losing when leaving a promotion/the business.
Double Juice	When both wrestlers bleed in a match.
Double-down	A point in the match where both wrestlers are bumped and selling.
Dud	A bad or boring match.
False Comeback	A spot in which the baby starts coming back but gets cut off/misses something.
False Finish	A move or spot that teases a finish.
Feed	Open yourself up to get hit.
Feeding	Getting up to be repetitively bumped.
Finish	The end of a match.
Fire	Incredible excitement that a babyface gets.
Gig Mark	A scar from blading.
Gimmick	(1) A wrestler's character. (2) Thing. (3) To do something.
Glob/Potato/Stiff	To hit someone hard.
Go Through	A time-limit draw.
Go Under	To lose.
Good Hand	A wrestler that promoters like.
Green	Someone in the business who is inexperienced.
Gusher	A deep cut that bleeds a lot.
Hard Way	To bleed without it being self-inflicted, usually unintentional.

Heat	(1) To have someone mad at you. (2) The time in a match where the heel beats up the face.
Heel	Villain/antagonist/bad guy.
Highspot/Spot	A piece of the match structure that brings the crowd up.
Hood	A wrestling mask.
Hopespot	A spot that shows the baby has some life left in him.
Hot Crowd	Loud, responsive crowd.
Hot Tag	When the fresh babyface is tagged in after a heat on the other baby.
House	Number of fans in the building.
Iggy/Office (Call)	A squeeze signal.
Jabroni	Slang term for jobber.
Job	To lose.
Jobber	Someone who loses.
Juice/Gas/ Chemical/Gear	Steroids
Kayfabe	(1) The wrestling code of silence. (2) Lie/hide. (3) Word telling other wrestlers to act.
Kill	Diminish.
Light	When a wrestler isn't stiff.
The Loop/Around the Horn	The trip to each town or series of towns that the promotion runs.
Loose	A wrestler who applies moves or holds lightly.
Mark	Wrestling fan.
Mark Out	When a mark gets excited about a wrestler, a spot, an angle, etc.
Married	Two wrestlers who have feuded with each other for a long time.
Mouthpiece	A manager who does the talking for a wrestler.
No Sell	When a wrestler stops selling moves.
Over	(1) To be liked. (2) To win.
Paying Dues	Doing whatever it takes to gain experience and learn.
Plant	Someone placed in the audience for a spot or an angle.
Pop	(1) Noise the crowd makes; applause. (2) To excite.

Program	Feud.
Promoter	The head of the wrestling organization.
Push	The process of getting a wrestler over (like a promotion).
Put Over	To "be put over" is to get the win. To "put someone over" is to do the job.
Receipt	The act of getting revenge.
Resthold	A submission hold that gives guys time to rest.
(Ring) Rat	A wrestling groupie.
Run	Have a wrestling show.
Run-in	Interference by a nonparticipant in a match.
Save	A run-in to protect a wrestler from being beat up after a match is over.
Screwjob	A finish with a controversial ending, often upsetting the fans.
Sell	Make something look believable (acting hurt).
Shine	To look good. (Babyfaces shine early on in a match.)
Shoot	Real.
Shooter	Someone who has a extensive shoot background (MMA, wrestling, etc.).
Showing Light	To unintentionally expose to the fans that the move did not connect.
Smark	A wrestling fan who thinks he or she has inside knowledge about the business, but doesn't.
Smart	A person who has the knowledge of the inner workings of the wrestling industry.
Smoz	Group of wrestlers involved in a pull-apart brawl.
Snug/Tight	Working very close to shoot.
Squash	A match where one wrestler dominates the entire match easily.
Stooge	A person who tells the promoter something that the wrestlers kept secret.
Strap	Championship belt.
Stretch	To legitimize a hold or holds on someone.
Swerve	When something that is incredibly shocking and unlikely happens.
Switch the Heat	To pass the blame onto someone else.

Take it Home/ Go Home	End the match.
Turn	When a face turns heel, or vice versa.
Tweener	A wrestler who is not quite a heel, but not quite a face.
Up	To win.
Wookie	A mentally handicapped mark.
Work	(1) Fake. (2) Pretend to make something look real. (3) Wrestle.
Worker	A wrestler.
Workrate	A wrestler's in-ring skill.

Index

About the Author

TED A. KLUCK is the author of *Facing Tyson: Fifteen Fighters, Fifteen Stories* (2006); *Paper Tiger: One Athlete's Journey to the Underbelly of Pro Football* (2007); and *Game Time: Inside College Football* (2007). His work has appeared in many of the most prominent sports publications, including: *ESPN the Magazine, Sports Spectrum Magazine,* ESPN.com Page 2, and several small literary journals. A bimonthly column for *Sports Spectrum Magazine* entitled "Pro and Con" won the Evangelical Press Association award for best standing column.